"New Hope Centre is like nothing else I have seen in Africa. Dr. Elizabeth Hynd is a Kingdom visionary who has seized the opportunity to help the displaced and forgotten children of Swaziland become the future spiritual leaders of their country. I encourage anyone who has given up on hope to read the inspiring story of courage, tenacity, and faith legacy of the Hynd family. It will lift your spirit and strengthen your faith in the God of the impossible."

—David Busic
Senior Pastor, Bethany First Church of the Nazarene

"Scripture tells us that we are to care for orphans and widows in distress. Dr. Elizabeth Hynd and her team at New Hope Center are the front line workers, being the hands and feet of Jesus Christ caring for the "abandoned and ignored" children in Swaziland. I pray that as you read this journey of faith that you will be compelled to take action and help. Together we can make a difference and bring glory to God while serving His children."

—Janine Maxwell
Co-founder of Heart for Africa
Author of *It's Not Okay With Me*

"This story has a happy ending because the Lord uses this ministry to bring hope where there is none in the lives of these children. He gives them beauty for ashes, joy instead of mourning. He makes them overcomers, and from that place of authority they are rising up with a testimony of salvation and restoration that is a blessing to their community, nation, continent, and the world. They also bring this testimony to Israel, and because they themselves have come out of a dark cold place to know the light and hope of Israel's Messiah, they have the authority to proclaim hope in Zion."

—Susan Knopman
Jerusalem House of Prayer for All Nations

"That children play an important role in the life and soul of any nation or family is beyond doubt. History from the time of Creation until the present day confirms this truth.

"Jesus Himself used children to illustrate and impress His hearers as to the importance of caring for children. Proof of this is that two books of the New Testament declare His displeasure as he rebuked the disciples with the words, 'Suffer the little children to come unto me and forbid them not for of such is the kingdom of God.'

"New Hope Centre and its staff remind us that the care of children is as important as ever. They are a practical demonstration of what God had in mind as they willingly give their lives to make a difference and bring life more abundantly to God's children at New Hope Centre in Swaziland. They deserve recognition through your support in spirit and in truth."

—Dr. Samuel W. Hynd
Veteran Missionary Doctor
Dr. Samuel W. Hynd, Commander of the British Empire
(awarded by Queen Elizabeth in honour of his work in the
Commonwealth of Britain)
BS (Rand), MB, ChB.(Glasgow), DTM & H(England)
(Degrees in medicine and tropical disease)
Member of Parliament
Minister of Health to the Kingdom of Swaziland

A Little Child
Shall Lead Them

A LITTLE CHILD
SHALL LEAD THEM

THE STORY OF SAVING A NATION

Dr. Elizabeth Hynd
with Gwen Ellis

WinePressPublishing
Your Book, Defined.

WinePress Publishing (PO Box 428, Enumclaw, WA 98022) functions only as book publisher. As such, the ultimate design, content, editorial accuracy, and views expressed or implied in this work are those of the author.

ISBN 13: 978-1-60615-041-2
ISBN 10: 1-60615-041-3
Library of Congress Catalog Card Number: 2010921258

CONTENTS

FOREWORD

The widespread outpouring of the Holy Spirit that we have been praying for will spring forth from the seed of hope within the heart of every believer. Within the pages of this book, you will meet many of the end-time ruling saints within the nation of Swaziland, Africa. God called the Hynd family into the nation of Swaziland many years past. God made places before He made people. He created the Garden of Eden for Adam and Eve, and I think it is certainly possible that God created the Hynd family for Swaziland.

It is my pleasure to introduce to you a fearless woman of God, Dr. Elizabeth Rose Hynd. Elizabeth is motivated by the impossible. She will cause the impossible to become possible. Elizabeth is a third-generation doctor within the Hynd family. God has challenged and called her to raise up an army of overcoming saints. This army is none other than today's Swazi orphans, who will become tomorrow's end-time ruling saints. Elizabeth is the keeper of the door of hope within the hearts of the orphaned children of New Hope Centre, located on Bethany Mountain in Swaziland, Africa.

The prophet Joel speaks about the future of a people such as today's orphans who live within New Hope Centre. Many of these end-time ruling saints are referred to today as orphans, but Elizabeth has seen them through the door of hope within her heart. She sees them as tomorrow's end-time ruling saints and leaders. Elizabeth Hynd is a general in God's end-time army. God has entrusted her to raise up a future end-time ruling army of saints from the outcast orphans of society within Swaziland. In Joel 2:2–5 and 9–11 (KJV), Joel refers to these people as "a great people and a strong; there hath not been ever the like, neither shall be anymore after it, even to the years of many generations. A fire devoureth before them and behind them a flame burneth: the land is as the garden of Eden before them, and behind them a desolate wilderness; yea, and nothing shall escape them. The appearance of them is as the appearance of horses; and as horsemen, so shall they run. Like the noise of chariots on the tops of mountains shall they leap, Like the noise of a flame of fire that devoureth the stubble, as a strong people set in battle array. . . . They shall run like mighty men . . . they shall march everyone in his ways, they shall not break ranks: a great people and a strong . . . The Lord shall utter his voice before his army for his camp is very great. . . ."

Elizabeth not only has a mandate from God to raise up a godly generation out of today's orphans within Swaziland, she also has an order from King Mswati, the King of Swaziland, to raise up godly leaders for tomorrow's world.

Within the pages of this book, you will read a true story about the Hynd Family, who came to Swaziland, Africa over a hundred years ago to medically and spiritually help the Swazi people and the Swazi nation. It is because of the obedience of the senior Dr. Hynd in answering God's call to go to Swaziland that we can tell the story about an overcoming nation which is now known throughout the world because of the AIDS epidemic. This small nation of Swaziland has known the touch of real love from the Hynd family. You are about to read a story about today's outcast orphans whom God has handpicked and destined to be tomorrow's glory carriers. You will read about God's heart for a nation and His plan to prepare a nation to host an end-time revival such as the world has never seen. This revival will take place in the future. It will happen in God's season and His time.

Elizabeth, it is no light thing for me to realize and acknowledge the friendship that I have found in you, and the favour you have within the Swazi nation—favour because of your faith and obedience to our heavenly Father, and because of your belief that one little Swazi will have the strength of one thousand, and that "a small nation will become a strong nation because the Lord our God will hasten it in His time" (Isa. 60:22).

You, Elizabeth, not only understand the anatomy of life, but you are willing to lay down your life to help the Swazi orphaned children into each new level that God has for their lives. It is with these things in mind that you are creating a hope for each child within New Hope Centre. It is with your attitude and mind-set that "a little child shall lead them," somewhere out there in the future that God has ordained for Swaziland. You must always remember that there will be a day when each orphaned child shall rise up and call you blessed. A little child shall surely lead you and the Swazi saints to open the door of hope to God's end-time outpouring within Swaziland. I am happy to call you my best friend and sister.

I believe that this book will stir your faith and motivate you, the reader, to rise up and do the impossible. The impossible is the very thing that excites you the most spiritually. Through a heartfelt relationship with our Heavenly Father and her hope for God's best in Swaziland, Elizabeth has produced what seems like the impossible. New Hope Centre is a home filled with love, laughter, joy, and excitement. It is the home of today's happy orphans, who will become tomorrow's Christian leaders.

Dr. Elizabeth Hynd is a modern-day Proverbs 31 woman. The difference between Elizabeth Hynd and the Old Testament Proverbs 31 woman is this: The Proverbs 31 woman "looketh at a field and buyeth it." Elizabeth looks at a mountain, and God gives it to her. She is a woman of utmost integrity. She is creating an individual hope for each and every child. It is with her attitude governed with a lively hope that Elizabeth accepts and raises today's orphaned, with the vision that today's orphan will be tomorrow's Christian leader.

They who sow in tears shall reap in joy. It is with the ebony and the ivory perfectly tuned on the piano that a triumphant song gives ear to victory. It is with the ebony and the ivory keys on the piano that the sound of praise, the sound of victory, and the sound of joy flows from Bethany Mountain in Swaziland, Africa, because "a little child" is being trained to lead the future generation into the Day of the Coming of the Lord. Our God reigns in the mountains of Swaziland.

—**June McKinney,** Director
New Hope Centre

INTRODUCTION:
JEDIDAH'S STORY

"There's a man at the gate. He's saying something about a child sitting under a tree somewhere," a staff member told me.

"I'll come now," I said. I walked to the strong sliding Rainbow gate that separates New Hope Centre from the outside world to greet the man. *"Shalom, Ukhala ngani?"* (Why are you troubled?)

"Ma'am, I have seen a very small child for five days. This child sits alone under a tree in the eastern part of the country. I see her every morning from the bus on my way to work. Can you help this child?"

"If the child is an orphan, we can help. Did you walk all the way up the mountain to tell me this?"

"Yes, Ma'am."

"Please come in and have some refreshment and tell me more about what you have seen."

The man told us that he could not help this child, as he had already taken in his nieces and nephews when their parents had died. He could not even afford to call New Hope Centre by phone to see if there was anything we could do. What he did was to walk the 1.7 kilometer up to our gate to tell us about her. The next day, two of our team members went with him to try to find the child. She was where the man had said. Our team members were in no way prepared for what they found. Under the tree sat a very little girl who looked to be no more than six months old. She was little more than a skeleton. Her back was bent, and her pelvic girdle appeared to have been distorted from sitting for such a long period of time. She was unable to walk or crawl. She was also unable to talk. She sat in her own excrement. How she had survived this long was a miracle. We asked people around the community about her, and found out that her entire family had died. A family had said that they would care for her, but sadly were unable to do so as she was so young and would have been too much trouble. Day after day, she sat under the tree, numb in her loneliness and eating handfuls of dirt to quiet the hunger pains. The team members bundled her up and brought her back to New Hope Centre. As soon as we had done the police registration for her, we took her straight to my father, Dr. Samuel Hynd, a veteran missionary doctor.

When he examined her, he was amazed to find she had a full set of teeth, and while she looked only a few months old, she had to be about two, given the number of teeth. "Another twenty-four to thirty-six hours and she would have been dead," he told us. An x-ray revealed that she had been eating handfuls of dirt to survive. We began to feed her, but it was no easy task. We soon learned that she could not chew, or even suckle, and for a while, everything she did manage to eat she would lose through her bowels in severe diarrhea. Her weakened, starved body could not handle real food.

Through a missionary friend in South Africa, we were able to take her for treatment at a hospital in Nelspruit to assess her bone and mental development. Only God's grace helped us jump the long queue and get in to see a specialist.

The physiotherapist wanted to test her crawling ability, but Jedidah didn't want to budge. So to get her to crawl, they put her beside my missionary friend, Heather, whose skin and hair is as white as snow. Jedidah wasn't a stranger to white people, as many of us at the home are white, but she had never seen someone as fair-skinned and light as Heather. She was terrified of her. Sure enough, when we put her down on the floor beside Heather, she crawled across the room as fast as she could go to *Make* (Mother) Wineli. So now we knew she could crawl if she wanted to.

We brought her home and began exercises to strengthen her muscles and bones in preparation for her to walk. Her bones were so fragile that they were unable to carry her body weight. But since she was the only one in the house who crawled, she wanted to stand and walk like everyone else—but that would mean broken bones. So we crawled along the passages with her when necessary so she could properly develop her psychomotor skills and neuron connections. Because she could not walk, of course, we had to keep her in diapers—something we were not used to. The older girls got involved in helping. In the beginning, Jedidah couldn't suck formula from a bottle, but she did know how to suck up food from a cup. We gave her a cup, and with some help, she was able to swallow her mashed-up food.

It took a long time and a lot of patient care and two broken bones before Jedidah was able to walk and to eat and speak. Slowly and consistently, God raised her up, and now she is a bright, healthy, happy child.

How does this happen—a child left alone under a tree? In Jedidah's case, one family member after another had died. People in the community tried to care for Jedidah, but due to their own circumstances were unable to continue their care. As a result, she was passed from one family to another. Finally, someone left her under a tree, where, but for the grace of God, she would have been bitten by a snake, chewed up and killed by a dog, eaten alive by the ants that will eat anything in their path, or raped. But none of that had happened. Again, it was God's grace and mercy that led the man to take a bus to our area and climb the hill from the highway to our home to tell us about this child, as he had no obligation to her.

It was the amazing grace of a loving Father. We named her Jedidah, which means "God's darling," and indeed she is surely that. God must have something very special in mind for little Jedidah. She runs around New Hope Centre chattering away to everyone in both SiSwati (her native language) and English. Jedidah is an example of just one of the many thousands of orphans in Swaziland who are forced to do almost anything to survive every day without hope, unless we are somehow led to them.

Swaziland is a small country with a population of roughly 950,000. Half of Swaziland's population has AIDS. Ten percent of the households are child-headed—orphans caring for orphans. There are reportedly 200,000 orphans in Swaziland (at time of writing), and the numbers continue to rise. What is to happen to these vulnerable children? How did Swaziland get into this deplorable condition? How can a country abandon its children? And how will it ever be redeemed and set on a new path? There is just one answer, and that answer is what this book is all about. And who knows? You may be part of Swaziland's solution.

PART I
THE CALLING

Chapter 1

In the Beginning

In the beginning of time, God established the nations of the earth and set boundaries around them. He saw fit to establish the Kingdom of Swaziland and nestle it in the beautiful mountains between the Lobombo mountain range and the Great African Escarpment. The Bantu peoples gradually migrated southward down the Indian Ocean coast with their herds of cattle, ever seeking fresh pastureland. When the Nguni people reached the mighty Pongola River, they turned westward through the gorge in the Lubombo Range and found the Southern tip of the Rift Valley, with plenty of water and great grasslands for their cattle.

The Swazi nation was birthed as different families and clans formed friendships and alliances under the leadership of the young founding King. This young King grew up herding his father's goats and cattle in the mountains of Swaziland. Then one night as he lay sleeping, he was visited by the Lord or an angel of the Lord from heaven. He was awakened out of a deep sleep, and the Lord spoke to him in a vision, explaining that a people with pointed noses and horsetail-like hair would be coming. These people would come bearing two objects—an *umculu* (which means "the book of the song") and an *indingilisa* (a circular button or a coin). The King asked what he was to do. The reply was to ignore the coin and to embrace the book. "Do not shed the blood of these people, but take the Umculu, the Word, and eat it on the inside, and the nation will live."

When His majesty awakened, he set in motion a plan of action that has made Swaziland one of the most peaceful Christian nations on the continent of Africa. The King called his people together and shared with his family and the whole nation what the Lord God had told him in the night. He told them of the vision he had had of the Lord of heaven and earth. King Somhlolo died before the people of the Book with pointed noses and horsetail-like hair came. It was his son who heard that such people had come, and he sent a regiment to go in search of them and bring them back with the *umculu* to teach the nation how to "eat the book on the inside so that the nation might live."

It was 1844 when the regiment of warriors sent by the King set off to find the people with the Book. Their search took them to the Methodist Mission at Thaba N'chu in the Free State, near Basutuland, as it was called in those days. Reverend Alison and two Lesotho evangelists returned with the warriors to Swaziland. The King received them and gave them a mountain to the south, called Mahamba, where the first church and mission station were established. The stone church where they began teaching the people about God's love is still used today.

At the time King Somhlolo had his vision, no one could ever have imagined that about two hundred years later, in the very place where he had his vision, a home for orphaned children, New Hope Centre, would be established. This is a place that would have made King Somhlolo's heart glad, for here orphaned children are not only being fed and sheltered, but they are nurtured in the Word of God. They are being trained to become the future leaders in Swaziland, especially now, as statistics show that by 2020, these young ones will be the elders in the nation. Children rescued from disease and despair are learning the life skills needed to succeed in their upcoming roles in leadership. Some are becoming champion swimmers; others are trained in ballet and music. All of these children who are being educated at the schools in New Hope Centre are being equipped to stand up for what they believe and to speak out in truth.

"Thanda Bantu"

One hundred years after King Somhlolo had his vision, Dr. David Hynd, his wife Knema, and their two small children arrived from Scotland to begin their lifelong ministry as medical and teaching missionaries to the gentle Swazi people. At that time, Swaziland was still a British protectorate that co-existed with the established Swazi monarchy. The Hynds met with the British High Commissioner, who took them to meet King Sobhuza II.

King Sobhuza II was an impressive man in stature and height. He reigned eighty-two years and nine months, and he was greatly loved by his people. Dr. Hynd appeared before the King and poured out his heart, telling him of his desire to serve the nation as a medical doctor. Dr. Hynd was a mathematician and philosopher teaching at Glasgow University, but God touched his heart one day after World War I as he read about the plight of the Swazi people. Swaziland was a nation stricken with typhoid and malaria, without a single medical doctor to help halt the death and sorrow. The British government had personnel and medical facilities for government servants only, and not for the common Swazi people. Dr. Hynd contacted the London foreign office and requested their assistance for his training to be a medical practitioner and tropical disease specialist, and for the support of his young family when they came to Swaziland to serve the nation. Dr. Hynd's wife, Knema, was a brilliant woman and a skilled teacher and preacher. Her heart was dedicated to enabling every Swazi to be equipped with the ability to read, meditate, and eat the Word of God so that the nation would live. The King was delighted with the Hynds' vision and commitment. He gave them a mountain close to what is now the city of Manzini, where they could teach, preach, and heal. They engaged themselves fully in this threefold ministry of Jesus.

The Hynds came to their mountain in an ox wagon. Once they arrived, they knelt down and blessed the land. Immediately, they rose up and began to build a mud-and-stone house. The verandah of that house became the first medical clinic and surgery in the land serving the Swazi people, while the kitchen became the first schoolroom. Their work for God, our Eternal King, had begun.

Even though Dr. Hynd was a gentle man, the Swazi people had little trust of white people or doctors. There was only a slim chance that any of the people would ever come to his patio clinic. So rather than sit and wait for them to come, Dr. Hynd got on his horse and rode out to the people's homesteads to offer his help. There, among the farmers and herdsmen, he began treating their malaria and typhoid. Often, he would arrive to find members of the family writhing on the floor, delirious with malarial fevers. Without treatment, they would have been dead within days. Typhoid also raged through the countryside, leaving people skinny and emaciated if they somehow survived the illness, and most did not. Homestead after homestead, he saw the freshly-dug grave mounds, and his heart broke with compassion for these people. Slowly, the

Swazi people began to trust him, and eventually gave him the name *Thanda Bantu* (lover of people). One of his first surgeries was the amputation of the leg of a small herd boy whose oxen pulled the slip—a tree stump—from off the sled. It ran over his leg, crushing it to a pulp.

Life in Swaziland for the Hynd family was challenging, and a far cry from the safety of their homeland of Scotland. But Swaziland was their home now, and the Hynds were never moved from their vision. They had dedicated their lives to this country, and they served the nation until their deaths. Today, they are both buried on the mountain King Sobhuza II gave them in Manzini.

Dr. Samuel Hynd

When David and Knema were gone, their work did not go unattended. As a young boy, their son, Samuel, had accompanied his father on his trips to the rural homesteads to visit and treat people. He was soon an apprentice assisting his dad by extracting teeth, stitching wounds, and learning diagnostic skills by intuition. Samuel gave his entire life and future to serve God and His kingdom when, at the age of thirteen, he surrendered his heart and life to Jesus. Step by step, he followed in his father's footsteps, taking medical training in South Africa and in Glasgow, Scotland. While he studied at the Royal School of Tropical Medicine in London, he met and married Rosemarie Ballard, a woman who was as committed to serving the Lord God as he was. She shared his calling and ministry until her tragic and untimely death in an automobile accident in Swaziland years later.

Samuel and Rosemarie Hynd came to Swaziland as newly-weds and joined David and Knema in the work. The medical challenges were now broadened to include smallpox and leprosy. Dr. David requested land from the British Government for a leper colony, and was given a mountain to the north of the capitol, in a place called Mbuluzi.

At that time, a cowgirl herding cattle far away in the mountains of Montana, USA, heard God calling her to become a nurse and care for lepers in Swaziland. Elizabeth Cole had no idea where Swaziland was, but knew she had been called. She redirected her life, became a nurse, and found her way to join Dr. David Hynd. She began to love and care for the rejected outcasts suffering the dreadful disease of leprosy. She gave her entire life as a gentle, humble, gracious, and loving nurse, riding her horse through the hills of Swaziland and caring for the maimed, estranged, and deformed victims of leprosy until it was finally eradicated during the years of Dr. Samuel Hynd's ministry. He was then able to transform the leper colony into an agricultural training centre for the Africa Christian Agricultural Trust. He is not only the founder, to this day he is still chairman of the trust. Dr. Samuel Hynd is now in his eighties and probably would have retired, but an even greater challenge than leprosy engulfed Swaziland. HIV/AIDS came to this mountain paradise in the late 1980s and has speedily become the number-one killer of Swazis. As he celebrated his eightieth birthday, Dr. Hynd, rather than retiring, set his sights on being a part of eradicating HIV/AIDS in the nation, and proclaimed as Caleb once did in Joshua 14:10–11, "So here I am today, eighty-five years old! I am still as strong today as the day Moses sent me out; I'm just as vigorous to go out to battle now as I was then. Now give me this hill country that the LORD promised me that day."

Dr. Elizabeth Hynd

I am the daughter of Dr. Samuel Hynd, and the granddaughter of Dr. David Hynd. I was born in Manzini, Swaziland, in the 350-bed hospital my grandparents built to replace their verandah clinic. The hospital today is fully equipped with an ICU unit and three operating theaters. While a teenager, my mother, Rosemarie Hynd, was killed in an automobile accident. My father grieved greatly. Even though he was devastated and was left with a broken heart and three daughters to raise, he did not waver in his love and commitment to the health and life of this nation. He continued his medical practice and served as the Cabinet Minister of Health for ten years under King Sobhuza II.

Growing up in Swaziland, I learned both English and SiSwati as a child playing with other Swazi children. I too accompanied my grandfather and father on medical trips to the fifteen rural health centers they established. I also accompanied my mother to rural areas to hold "church" each Sunday, sitting on grass mats under the lofty jacaranda trees. I did my early years of education in Swaziland, but later went to schools in the US and the UK before heading back to South Africa for my university education. I loved learning, but had no intention of taking up the family practice of medicine, as my parents and grandparents had worked extensively long hours each day, from my observation.

I attended thousands of church services in my youth and listened to multitudes of messages, but it was only while I was at the Witwatersrand University in Johannesburg that God touched my heart.

Being raised on the mission field is a tough and challenging experience, and one where the rubber hits the road, so to speak. I grew up knowing the Word of God and understanding the ways of the Lord as few children ever have the privilege of doing. I loved the Word of God. It contained such wisdom and love that reading and studying it was my delight and confidence. I memorized several entire books such as Isaiah and Ezekiel.

Growing up, I lived on a mission station that had many different nationalities and personalities, all of whom claimed to be living for the same Lord and Savior. They claimed that the

Holy Spirit lived in them, but their attitudes and actions did not match the Holy Spirit whom I read about in the scriptures. I had difficulty reconciling that it was the same Holy Spirit who led them as the Holy Spirit of the Bible. The two did not reconcile in my understanding, and so I decided that although the God of the Bible was great and wonderful, I was not sure that that God was the same God of the Christians I observed.

Assailed by Doubt

I was assailed by doubt when, as an avid reader of the Word of God, I found that the Holy Spirit described and introduced there was wonderful, while the Holy Spirit who was manifested in many Christians' lives was vastly different in nature and character from that written in the Word. As I pondered this about the age of seven, I could not decide which Holy Spirit was the real one—the one written in the Word of God or the one demonstrated in the lives of believers.

One day, I shared with my father that I could not resolve this conflict of revelation, so I was choosing no longer to identify myself as a Christian. Dr. Samuel, with much wisdom, did not argue with me, but respected my choice and asked me to respect his choice and commitment. We pledged on those conditions, and life went on. By the time I started university, I was defining myself as an atheist, and did much destruction in the lives of others who called themselves Christian but who did not know what their Bibles really said. I could argue for hours with people and demonstrate the shakiness of their faith and commitment until many doubted themselves. I believed that few Christians truly laid a foundation in their lives on the Word of God, His thoughts, or His ways.

At university I was reading the sciences, studying biology, microbiology, chemistry, and physics, and it was at that time the God of all creation began wooing me. I began to ponder and wonder at the perfection of all I studied and the immense beauty in everything. Slowly He began to reveal Himself through His creation. The perfection and splendor of the cells, molecules, microbes, and all that exists held testimony to me that all this could not be a random happening. I began to believe in my heart that there must be a Supreme Being who was all-intelligent, or as the Bible says, "omniscient." Then, slowly, I began to realize that this Creator, whoever He or It was, had to be immensely loving, because only great, great love could produce such awesome beauty in all these cells, crystals, atoms, and molecules. I came to believe that there had to be a supreme being, a Creator of great wisdom and tremendous love.

Life was not easy, and I began to erode into believing that all of life was painful. All I seemed to do was to hurt the people I loved and cared about, and all they seemed to do was to hurt me, even though they claimed to love me. So I decided that the best thing to do was to commit suicide, and I spent some time researching how to do this effectively so that there was no chance of being rescued and brought back to life. It had to be a once-and-for-all happening. But the God who had created me and formed me in my mother's womb knew my thinking. He began to work in my spirit, and I began to question the logic of suicide. I came to the logical conclusion that if I had not had the right to choose to come into the world, then I also did not have the legal or moral right to remove my existence from the world. So rather than commit suicide, I concluded that it was best to leave society and live as a beachcomber on some deserted African beach, where I could hurt no one and no one could hurt me.

I told no one of my plan, but I closed my bank account, bought a plane ticket and prepared to leave. The day I was to depart, a friend dropped in for a cup of coffee. She was a Christian Sunday school teacher who knew little of the Word of God. To get rid of her, I embarked on a complex debate with her about some technical faith issues. I thought it was the best way to exasperate her and cause her to leave my apartment so I could leave without anyone knowing where I had gone.

God Shows Up

During the course of the arguments, I decided to refer to my Bible and show my friend the problem in her theology. I took up my Bible and opened it. As the page fell open, I saw flames moving across the page, as if an invisible hand was writing in cursive one word at a time: *For God so loved the world that he gave his only begotten Son, that whosoever believes in Him shall not perish but have everlasting life.* I shut the book. I couldn't believe what I'd seen and read. Then I randomly opened it again. The same phenomenon occurred. I shut it again, thinking, *This is strange. I do not drink alcohol, I do not take drugs, I have had a reasonable amount of sleep, and I have a scientifically trained mind, so I don't hallucinate or daydream.* I opened the Bible a third time, and the same phenomenon was repeated. I then fell on my knees, for I knew God was speaking directly to me through the word of the verse written in fire on the page the Gospel of John, chapter 3, verse 16.

In that moment, I answered the Creator of heaven and Earth, the Creator of Elizabeth Rose Hynd. I said, "Surely, if you love me enough to take this scientific mind and penetrate its highly-trained reality to get this message to me personally, then you truly do love me, and I need to be loved like this."

I then asked my friend to pray with me. She stayed late and left some time during the night. I prayed and wept through the entire night, confessing and repenting all my sins of thought, word, and deed, both my actions and my inactions. In the morning, as the sun rose, I realized that I had become a Christian. I knew that the next thing I needed to do was to find a church family, as the Word requires us to fellowship together. But how could I choose a church, when it appeared that so many of them fall short of the glory of God? The God who saved me is faithful, and He led me radically as I radically dedicated my life to doing whatever he wanted me to do. I was ready to serve the King of kings with all my heart, soul, and body.

I had learned the scriptures long before I committed myself to Jesus. I knew and loved the story of Paul the Apostle. His had been a life of adventure, uncertainty, frustration, and a deep abiding love of the One who had called him so dramatically through his Damascus Road experience. Once Paul met the Savior on that road, he never looked back. And after my "Damascus Road" experience, I never looked back.

During certain periods of Paul's life, he had cared for his personal financial needs by working as a tentmaker. That sounded like a good plan to me. While I was totally committed to God's plan for my life, I confess that I hoped He would allow me to be a tentmaker missionary so that I did not have to live by faith. Coming from a long line of missionaries, I knew what living by faith was all about, and I really didn't want to live that way. Even though I realized my life would have its seasons of plenty and those of want, I hoped it might not have to be as challenging as it had been for my parents and grandparents.

Japan

I completed graduate school at Peabody College and Vanderbilt University in Nashville, Tennessee, with master's and Ph.D. degrees. It was in May that I finished my final examinations and the oral defense of the dissertation for the Ph.D. As I sat one beautiful spring day, I thanked the Lord for the wonderful life I had. I was minister of youth to more than two hundred fifty junior high children. I was doing outreach to hundreds of children each week in the housing estates. I had a weekly puppet show on TV. And I was teaching in two different universities in Nashville and in a high school.

I had completed my degrees in two years, and God had provided for tuition fees and a home to live in. Everything in my life was great, but I found myself saying to Him that there has to be more to life than this. I told Him that I wanted to enter into life in Christ to the fullest. I discussed with the Lord how I wanted to be free of every earthly culture and way of thinking. I wanted to be fully spiritually-minded. I discussed with Him how (at least to my understanding) the best way I could truly re-examine every thought, pattern, habit, expectation, and attitude in life was to go somewhere where I would experience severe culture shock. All I needed to know was where to go to experience that kind of culture shock so that it would turn my world inside out. As I pondered this, I thought of the continents and nations I had visited, loved, prayed for, or known through friends. I realized that Japan was the one nation I knew very little about—petite women, the Hiroshima atomic bomb, Pearl Harbor, and not much more.

I had lived in Africa, Europe, and North America. I had traveled in the Middle East and South America. As a child, I had been fascinated by China, Thailand, Burma, Tibet, Kashmir, and India, and had read and studied extensively about them. The only country I knew virtually nothing about was Japan. I went to the placement office at the university to look for a position in Japan. I was about to experience an amazing leading of the Lord.

As I paged through the files in the placement office, I found a job in my field in Japan. I applied, even though it was then May, and the closing date for the application had been in March.

I received an immediate reply and an offer of a three-year contract. I hastily answered that I couldn't sign a three-year contract because I was not sure I would like being in Japan. I needed to go on a year-by-year basis. I was writing to request if I could sign for one year, with the option to renew at the end of that first year. They agreed.

I completed my dissertation, held my oral defense, flew to Africa to see family and friends, flew back to the United States to pick up my dissertation and make one change in one paragraph, submitted it, and flew onward to Japan to begin teaching in the fall.

In Japan, I taught and ministered to students the Good News and the love of Jesus through Bible classes on Sunday afternoons and evenings. I worked with a wonderful Mennonite couple who had been in Japan serving the Lord for many years, Dr. and Mrs. Friesen. I was making a considerable sum of money, and I was happy there, as God had put a great love for the Asian people in my heart. I am only five feet, two inches tall, with narrow eyes, and at that time I had straight black hair. If I wore my makeup just right, I could pass for a Japanese woman. I felt I belonged in Asia.

As planned, I went year-to-year on the contract, and after two years, when the third contract came to my desk, I asked the Lord what to do—renew it or leave. The Lord spoke plainly and said, "This is the last contract you will sign." So I signed it and finished three years in Japan. All that year, I searched for suitable positions elsewhere by first analyzing my skills and interests, and then searching for suitable matches. I was interviewed and short-listed for three excellent jobs, but when I received three letters offering me three positions, my heart did not "smile." There was no rejoicing. I turned each offer down with a humble apology. In May of the last year, it became urgent that I find direction, as my visa in Japan would expire on the tenth of June and I would have to leave. I did not know where to go.

A friend was on her way to the UK for an International Educators conference. I asked her to take an abbreviated version of my vitae to post on the wall at the conference, just to see what might happen. Soon, I received a call from a Christian Lutheran school in Hong Kong. They wanted a science educator with my qualifications and experience, who was a Christian and would not promote evolution. I accepted the position over the phone, and this time my heart smiled. I knew that this was the way and I was to walk in it, as the scripture says (Isa. 30:21).

I packed up, shipped my few belongings to Hong Kong, and arrived before the shipment did. I found an apartment in the seaside village of Stanley on the south side of Hong Kong Island, and arranged for it to be painted and made ready for me to move in as soon as my things arrived.

By this time in my life, I realized that I had accomplished most of my dreams. So I told God that He could now have the rest of my life to do with as He pleased. I had explained earlier that my objective in going to Japan was to "turn my world inside out," and it was accomplished. Everything in Japan was different—blood is considered dirty, so how can your sins be washed away by the blood of Jesus? When you use a handsaw in Japan, the teeth are the opposite direction to handsaws in the west. Honor is given by bowing down with the deepest humility, and so it goes. I learned to speak, read, and write Japanese to a grade eight level. I learned to play the *Koto*, took *Sumie* painting lessons, and travelled from north to south and east to west, staying in quaint Japanese inns. Truly, every thought, assumption, belief, and attitude was challenged while I maintained a pursuit of study and meditation on God's Word and waited upon Him to know increasingly His thoughts, His ways, and His love.

In Hong Kong, life changed dramatically. I went from the affluence and prestige of campus life in Japan to the dregs of humanity in the slums of Hong Kong. I went from safety to danger. I passed from an ordered and peaceful life to one of the unbelievable excitement of never knowing what might happen next, or when God would show up with a supernatural intervention and miracle—the lame walking, the blind seeing, the sick healed, and prisoners to drugs, gambling, prostitution, and mental illness set free. But that is a story for the next chapter.

Chapter 2

THE ELEPHANT ON THE BUS

With the Lord's clear direction to move to Stanley Village on Hong Kong Island, I was ready for the next chapter in life. I spent the rest of the summer flying around the world on a "round-the-world ticket." I visited all my friends scattered all over the globe: Singapore, Delhi, South Africa, Swaziland, England, America, and back to Hong Kong to be welcomed with the stifling humid heat of the Orient.

The first Saturday after I arrived in Hong Kong, I needed to go to Kai Tak airport on the mainland to meet a friend coming from Japan, who was to visit for a few days. As I did not know my way around, I decided to take the public bus system. I left very early to make sure I was at the airport before my friend arrived.

As I boarded the big, blue double-decker bus, I saw a white lady with blonde hair getting on. I decided to sit with her so I could learn a little about living and surviving in Hong Kong. Everyone else on the bus was obviously Chinese, and I did not know one word of Chinese. This lady and I began to talk, and as we talked, my heart warmed within me. I felt sure she was a Christian, so I asked her, and she said yes. Then I asked where she worshipped, and she said she did not go to church. Now that was interesting. I asked her what she did instead, and she explained about her ministry among the Triads (gangsters), drug addicts, and prostitutes.

I was thrilled, and told her I believed that what she was doing was real Christianity. She invited me to accompany her to her meeting place—The Well, as she called it. As I was very early for the flight I was meeting, and The Well was right near the airport, I decided to go with her. And so I entered the infamous Walled City for the first time.

The Walled City can be traced back to the Song Dynasty, China's ruling dynasty between 960 and 1279. The area served as a watch post for defending the Kowloon Peninsula against pirates. It was also a place for managing the production of salt. After ceding Hong Kong to the British in 1842, the Chinese authorities believed it was necessary for them to have a military/administrative post in Hong Kong to rule the area and to keep British influence from spreading. The post was agreed upon, and China established the Walled City as a place where the Chinese could keep troops, as long as they did not interfere with Britain's temporary rule.

Britain quickly went back on this unofficial part of the agreement, and attacked the Walled City in 1899. But when they went in, they found it deserted. They walked away from the post and thus left the ownership of Kowloon's Walled City up in the air. No one owned it. It became a curiosity and a tourist attraction, because there, tourists could see a bit of old China.

In 1940, during WWII, Japan occupied Hong Kong. By this time, the Walled City had become inhabited. The Japanese evicted people living there and then demolished much of it, including the surrounding wall, to provide building materials for the nearby Kai Tak Airport.

After Japan's surrender and abandonment of the Walled City, it wasn't long before squatters and disadvantaged people moved in. Britain tried to drive them out, but to no avail. Since the wall had been torn down much earlier, there was nothing to protect the Walled City from evil influence. It became a haven for crooks and drug addicts. The Hong Kong Police could not enter the city as they had no rights there, because it technically belonged to China. Thousands of refugees poured into the Walled City when the People's Republic of China was founded in 1949.

No one took care of the place. Britain had adopted a "hands-off" policy. The area was ruled by gangs called Triads. The Triads were gangs of thugs who dealt dope, promoted prostitution, controlled local businesses, counterfeited everything from handbags to published books, and engaged in every kind of illegal activity known to man. The Triads were, and still are, powerful in Hong Kong. Murder, mayhem, illicit sex, and every distortion of basic humanity ran rampant everywhere within the Walled City. It was into this place of darkness that I ventured on my way to the airport, accompanied by the "Angel of the Walled City," as she is known there. It was an area of vice, poverty, violence, drug dens, filth, and squalor such as I had never seen in my life.

Then we stepped from the filthy alleyways into a brilliantly-lit whitewashed room, The Well. Inside, men were praying for one another and casting out demons. Some were engaged in more "normal" activities, such as practicing guitars. As I watched, tears rolled down my cheeks, for this was the church my heart had been longing for. I had known that it must exist somewhere in the world, but I had never before seen or known church like this—such love, such grace, such humility, such faith.

I could not stay for the whole evening service, as I still had to get to the airport, but this wonderful woman gave me her card and said they had a Bible study on Sunday afternoons that was translated into English, if people wanted to come. I looked down at the card. Her name was Jackie Pullinger. At the time, her name didn't mean anything to me. I had never heard of her, never read her book, *Chasing the Dragon*, and certainly was not looking for her. What I did not know was that I had just met an amazingly famous woman. Finding her had been something like finding the proverbial needle in the haystack. I was elated as I went to meet my friend from Japan in Kai Tak airport.

The next morning my friend and I went to the Anglican (Episcopal) Saint John's Cathedral for the family service and communion. During the passing of the peace, I greeted one couple who were obviously visitors. Having lived in the city ten days, I felt very much able to welcome visitors and share my limited knowledge and experience. Then they asked me an amazing question. "Do you have any idea how to find Jackie Pullinger?"

"Oh yes," I told them with great delight. "I met her last night, and here is her card." Immediately after finishing our lunch together, we went and phoned her, asking directions to the Bible study. That afternoon at the Bible study, I wept buckets of tears. Jackie came to ask why I was weeping, and I told her how I had longed to know the *Church*, and how although I had grown up as a Christian and had attended more services in my life than I could ever count, I recognized that this church—the one here in the Walled City—was what Jesus prayed and talked about in John 17. Jackie prayed for me and released me into the power of the supernatural gifts of the Holy Spirit.

I continued teaching at the Lutheran school, but also started taking students to the streets to minister the love and power of

God to street people and drug addicts. We worked weekends with drug addicts, spending a great deal of time with them as we prayed for them Saturday nights at The Well in the Walled City. During the week we visited street-sleepers, prostitutes, and drug addicts, and got to know the streets of Hong Kong Island. There was never enough time in a day to do all that we wanted to do. Finally, I could not juggle my two lives of teaching and evangelizing. So I quit my tent-making job of teaching. From that day to this, I have served the Lord by faith.

Jackie—Poon Soo Je

Jackie Pullinger is one of those heroes of the faith who stepped out and did what God told her to do. It all began when she was a five-year-old child, and a missionary came to her Sunday school class. The missionary was a lady who wore a long dark skirt and had her hair in a proper bun. After her talk, the missionary asked, "Could God want you on the mission field?" It was a question that stuck in Jackie's mind, even as her practical side said, "Of course God wants me on the mission field. God wants everyone on the mission field." That subtle question stayed with her through her teen years, through her boarding school years, and through music school. She nurtured the question through teasing from friends and through parties that were both sordid and boring. One night, she had a dream that she and her family were studying a world map on the dining room table. As they studied Africa, she saw a pink-colored country (pink is her favorite color), and the label of the country was Hong Kong. In her dream, they talked about how strange it was that Hong Kong was in Africa. She woke up pondering the dream. She thought, *Well, all missionaries go to Africa.*

Then one day, she was on the way home on a commuter train when she met two friends. They took her to a flat where a gentleman was talking about the Bible. These young people were not the long-skirted, bun-wearing type of Christians. They were vibrant and alive and "normal." It was there that she learned that no one can go to God except through Jesus. She gave her life, once and for all, to Jesus. Her life began to expand rapidly.

She started teaching music, but now that Christ had entered her life, she wanted to give her life wholly to Him. She began to think once again about missionary life. She wrote to some missionary groups. They didn't want her unless she could teach English and math. Music was too much of a luxury for them at that point. She contacted the Ministry of Overseas Development to find out about a teaching position. They had no jobs for musicians. She wrote her old missions society. They wrote back, saying they would not accept her until she was twenty-five years of age.

Finally, in a prayer group, God spoke to her prophetically telling her, "Go. Trust me and I will lead you." But she did not know where to go. Finally, she got some advice from a minister she had known for a while. He told her, "If I were you, I would go out and buy a ticket for a boat going on the longest journey you can afford, and pray to know where to get off." His additional advice consisted of listening hard to see how God would lead on that trip.

She counted her money and learned that she had enough to go from France to Japan on a ship. It would certainly give God time to speak with her about where she should serve Him. She could get off the ship when she was sure God had spoken, or she could stay on and go all the way back to England. One can only imagine the protest and questions thrown at her by family and friends. Even her old missionary society cast doubt over her enthusiasm. But in time, she did leave her homeland on a ship. She stayed onboard until the ship docked in Hong Kong harbor. For a while it appeared that she would not be able to leave the ship because she had no job and no money, and knew no one in the city. Then God reminded her of a policeman she knew who lived in Hong Kong, and since policemen were highly revered, she gave the authorities the policeman's name and was allowed to disembark.

Jackie's first venture into the Walled City came when a woman invited her to visit her nursery school and church. The lady didn't tell her what she would face inside the Walled City, and up until the time she arrived at the city, Jackie thought she was going to a quaint Chinese walled village that you might find described in a guide book. She was not. She followed her guide behind tawdry shops, through narrow gaps between the shops, and down slime-covered passageways. It was dark, and smelled of rotten food, excrement, offal, and rubbish. Above the streets, the houses on each side of the alley almost touched, shutting out all sunlight from above. Here was a plastic flower factory, and there was an aged prostitute who had bought several children whom she prostituted instead of herself. Then she passed a restaurant that captured and cooked dogs, and next, a pornography theater. Yet among the dregs of human life, some people were trying to eke out a legitimate living. Children were trying to go to school. Some of these children would live their whole lives in this horrid place.

By the time she went into the Walled City for the second time, Jackie had an unusual experience—joy—the giddy kind of joy you feel on your birthday. She had first felt that kind of joy at her confirmation, and again when she accepted Jesus into her life. Now here it was again in this profane place. It didn't make sense, except that God often doesn't seem to make sense from an observer's point of view.

That was the beginning of Jackie's forty years of ministry to the poor and neglected of Hong Kong's society inside the Walled City until it was torn down in 1992. Others had tried and failed to bring the Gospel message to this corner of the earth, but Jackie, in humility and more than a little naïveté, went in and started living among the people. Equipped with a childlike faith and complete dependence on the Holy Spirit, she was soon known throughout the city by triad gang leaders, prostitutes, and those who operated and frequented drug dens.

When I joined Jackie at that meeting at The Well, I had no idea who she was and how knowing her would radically change my life and prepare me for future ministry. I did not know that I would be working with this pioneer among missionary woman for the next twelve years of my life. All I knew was that when I first went to The Well, I had a sense of belonging. I had never seen anything like what she was doing. People were being radically delivered from addiction and darkness in a way that confounded any social worker or theory. Not only were these men and women delivered from heroin and opium through prayer, but they were praying in a heavenly language and delivering others from the same bondages from which they had been freed just moments before. It was the most challenging and rewarding work of my life. Every day I saw the reality of God in powerful ways, and the joy it brought me was "joy unspeakable and full of glory," as the song goes.

One of my first experiences was going to visit street people one afternoon. We had such amazing experiences out on the street. I was having lunch with a Chinese businessman who wanted to know why my Christian life was so vibrant and happy compared to others. I asked him what God could do to prove to him that He is alive and well. He answered, "If I saw the life of a street-sleeper changed." (Street people are called street-sleepers in Hong Kong.) I took up the challenge and said, "Come, we will buy three take-away rice boxes, find three street people, and see what God does." We walked the streets, found one dirty, smelly man, gave him lunch, asked him if we could bless him and the food, then we prayed for him and moved on to the second man. When we came to the third man and gave him his take-away rice-and-chicken lunch, we asked if we could pray for him and bless him like the others. He agreed. When I started to pray over him in tongues, he became very still. We prayed for quite awhile. I knew no Chinese at that stage, so I had to have the scenario translated for me by the businessman. When the man finally opened his eyes, I asked him what had been happening. He said a man came to him, dressed in white clothes. I asked if the man spoke to him. He said yes, and that His name was Jesus and He wanted to be this street person's Friend. Then I asked how he had responded to Jesus. The man had told Jesus that he did not know how to be a friend to anyone, as he had never had a friend. Jesus replied that he would be a Friend to him. Jesus would walk with him and talk with him and never leave him, and that way he too would learn how to be a friend. I asked if the man wanted such a Friend. He said yes, and I told him that Jesus was my Friend too, and I could introduce him. I then led him in the sinner's prayer for salvation. We arranged to meet the man every week for lunch and Bible study.

This Chinese businessman came with me each week to visit the man. We sat on the pavement and shared lunch and the Word of God together. The transformation of this man's life through Christ was amazing. The businessman became a Christian, and his life was changed so dramatically that his family became Christians. Eventually, the businessman's family asked if the old man from the street could come and live with them and be their adopted grandfather. The old man lived with them from that time on. The children in the family taught him to read, and the old man created an atmosphere of love and friendship around himself. Every day in the park, a gathering of several hundred old Chinese people would attend "church" taught by this illiterate old man—a former street-sleeper. He was transformed by the work of the Holy Spirit in his life. He gave love and wisdom through the Word, and he brought healing and relief from suffering for many through the miracle-working power of the Holy Spirit. This was one of many amazing stories of lives transformed as we ministered to the poor. They, in turn, began to announce the coming of the Kingdom of God in ways explained in scripture: "Not many of you were wise by human standards; not many were influential; not many were of noble birth" (1 Cor. 1:26). "We have done so not according to worldly wisdom but according to God's grace" (2 Cor. 1:12). Jackie's theme for years was that the "poor" are the many who will announce the Kingdom of God, and this story was a clear demonstration of that truth.

The Elephant on the Bus

One day during my time in Hong Kong, I was riding a city bus and reading an article about elephants. Since I had grown up in Africa, I had seen many elephants and I already knew a lot about them. I had spent much time with graduate students at the University of Witwatersland, sharing in their research on the life and health of elephants. But on this day, tears began to roll down my cheeks as I was reading. What was this about? Why was I weeping over an article about elephants?

"Father God, what is happening?" I asked.

"I'm touching your heart for Africa," He answered.

"That's great, Lord, I will begin praying for Africa," I told Him; and I did.

A couple of years went by, and once again I was riding on a Hong Kong City bus and reading a book on Africa's gentle giants. The book was entitled *Keepers of the Kingdom,* and it told how the elephant is one of nature's best conservationists. The book told of the elephant's vital role in Africa's survival for thousands of years; how the elephant prepares water pans to collect rainwater, a drinking hole for the other animals and so on. Again, I found tears streaming silently down my face as I read.

This time, I knew God was asking more of me than just my prayers. I knew He was calling me back to the land of my birth. I didn't want to leave Asia. After traveling the world and living in many countries, Asia had become my first love. It was home. Now God was calling me to Africa. I didn't want to go, but I had walked with God long enough to know it was He who was calling, and when He calls, we must answer. His voice had guided me most of my life. He has been—and is—my closest Friend. God is so patient with us when we struggle with His will. He was patient with me now. I told Him I didn't want to go, but that I would go when He had made my heart ready. God was about to do that. He was about to take my tears over African elephants and turn them into compassion for orphaned children in Africa. I was about to become a mother to a nation.

Chapter 3

THE DEBORAH CALL

I was in a taxi one day when I got the call to Africa—and I mean I literally got the call in the taxi, on my phone pager (there were no cell phones in those days). It was my father, inviting me to come to Kuala Lumper, Malaysia, where he and Swaziland's King Mswati III were at the Commonwealth Head of State meeting, where the King was to give a speech. He told me I should come right away and meet with them. I flew immediately to Malaysia.

Each morning, before the meetings and deliberations began, the King would call his delegation together for prayer. It was in one of those prayer meetings that the King asked me to consider returning to Swaziland to give my talents and gifts to the nation. Now I had a double call. God had spoken to me loudly and clearly on the Hong Kong City bus while I was reading a book about African elephants, and now the King of Swaziland was asking me personally to come back to Swaziland to serve the kingdom. It was a call from the King of kings and from the King of Swaziland. Now the time had come.

I had many responsibilities in Hong Kong, and it took some time to wrap things up before I could leave. Then, in a dream one night, I found myself walking on the street, and God told me to turn to my left. Immediately to my left was the glass door of a travel agent's office. The Lord told me it was time for me to buy my ticket and go back to Africa. The next morning, I bought my ticket. I arrived in Swaziland just in time for the Somhlolo Festival of Praise (the annual celebration of giving thanks for the coming of the Word of God through King Somhlolo's vision), to begin a new chapter in my life. While it had been difficult to leave Asia, by the time I arrived in Africa, my heart was ready.

The Swaziland I grew up in and the one I returned to were very different. In this Swaziland, people were dying. People in their twenties and thirties would be full of life one day, and the next they would start to get sick; soon, they wasted away to nothing, until they finally died. Even worse, the nation was in denial about what was happening. And this was only the beginning. No one could have anticipated the devastation that was on its way. But there were signs, signs many chose to ignore, and all those signs pointed toward HIV/AIDS—a virus that was starting to ravage many neighboring countries. Swaziland was not to be an exception.

As I began working with different ministries around Swaziland, I tried to talk about AIDS with the pastors and medical personnel, but many simply brushed my concerns aside. It was as though there was a shroud around this deadly virus. It was a shroud of shame and silence about a disease that was infecting all spheres and every strata of society—including the royal family.

Now back in Swaziland, I joined a church called Christian Family Centre, which met in a tent and had a ministry to the poor who lived on the garbage dumps. The pastor's name was Zakes Nxumalo. One day, my prayer and worship leader partner, Lulu Nxumalo, invited me to a meeting where June McKinney was preaching. The shroud that covered Swaziland was about to be torn away.

Dr. June McKinney, a prophetic minister from Florida, USA, was in Swaziland at the invitation of His Majesty, King Mswati III. God had called June out of her profession as a surgical nurse in 1984 to go to the streets and red-light districts of cities around the USA to administer healing, not of the medical kind but of a spiritual kind, to drug addicts and prostitutes. She started locally in Jacksonville, Florida, but soon she went to major cities across the United States. Later, the Lord called her to minister to heads of state and leaders in other nations. Later on, one day, during a time of prayer over a globe, God told her to go Swaziland, as He wanted her to give King Mswati III a message from heaven's throne room. She had never heard of Swaziland, and God even spelled the King's name for her. She had to go to a library and look up the country in an atlas. In obedience, she came alone to Swaziland in 1989 for three days. God amazingly opened doors for her to meet King Mswati III and give him in person the message from the King of kings to the King of Swaziland.

Her message was that King Mswati III was a man chosen by God. He knew God's heart, and he needed to know God's power. When she prayed over him, tongues of fire from heaven enveloped both of them. Thereafter, His Majesty invited June two or three times a year to minister to and teach the Royal family. Later He invited her to speak at the national Good Friday and Resurrection Sunday services in the national stadium to tens of thousands of people. Since then, she has ministered to the church throughout Swaziland, from north to south and east to west. Through her prophetic calling, a new move of prayer and worship has been established in the nation in preparation for the soon-coming, God-appointed time of national revival. God's promise to her is found in Isaiah 55:5 (KJV): *Behold thou shalt call a nation that thou knowest not, and nations that knew not thee shall run unto thee because of the Lord thy God, and for the Holy one of Israel; for He hath glorified thee.*

In 1998, June came to Swaziland at the invitation of King Mswati III for the national celebration of the 30th anniversary of the nation's independence from Britain, and also of the King's 30th birthday. June's message was on the "Password of Praise" taken from Psalm 89:15: *Blessed are the people who know the passwords of praise and shout on parade in the bright presence of God* (The Message). This was a teaching I had never heard anyone share before, but it was a teaching that the Lord had revealed to me years before. It was one of the keys to my walk with Him. I was thrilled and overjoyed to hear in June McKinney the same message. I introduced myself immediately after the service. What a joy and delight to meet someone of like revelation and understanding!

As we talked after the message, I shared my total delight in hearing such a revelation. What she said meant that she had a relationship with the Lord similar to mine. Later, I discovered she had worked in the streets of Jacksonville with street people, drug addicts, and prostitutes—even having them live in her home during their time of restoration. She had then gone to other USA cities with a bus and a team to minister. So we had walked a similar path of ministering to those who were enslaved by sin—she in the USA, and I in Hong Kong. We knew well the heart of God and the power of the hope that lived in us.

During the message, God had been speaking to her about who I was in the spirit realm. Now she began to prophesy over me and my life. From that moment on, we became sisters in the Lord. We were fellow pilgrims, and since June is a platinum blonde and I had jet black hair, we joked about being the ebony and the ivory of the keys of the piano that could make a joyful and powerful sound of praise on the earth, and that could raise a battle shout to establish the Kingdom of Glory on earth. I went to every service where she preached during the two weeks she was in Swaziland.

Earlier, June was walking up the main street in Manzini, Swaziland, when the Lord spoke to her and said, "I want you to build an orphanage here in Swaziland." He said that the home would be used for His glory in the coming revival and the end time here in Swaziland. At that time, AIDS had not hit Swaziland in the prevalent sweep of despair that came later. June said, "The Lord further instructed me that the orphanage would be His instrument in raising up a future generation of warriors who would not bend or bow to the traditions of men. The Lord said the children that He would send to the orphanage would be hand-picked by Him and only Him." This stirred June, and brought to mind the words in Isaiah 5:26–29 (KJV):

> He will lift up an ensign to the nations from far, and will hiss unto them from the end of the earth: and, behold, they shall come with speed swiftly:
>
> None shall be weary nor stumble among them; none shall slumber nor sleep; neither shall the girdle of their loins be loosed, nor the latchet of their shoes be broken:
>
> Whose arrows are sharp, and all their bows bent, their horses' hoofs shall be counted like flint, and their wheels like a whirlwind:
>
> Their roaring shall be like a lion, they shall roar like young lions: yea, they shall roar, and lay hold of the prey, and shall carry it away safe, and none shall deliver it.

Though she tried, it was very difficult for June to do anything concerning the home until we met a couple of years after the Lord had first spoken to her about it. Once we met, the Lord worked His will to establish that which He had revealed by His Spirit for the nation of Swaziland, and that which He has now revealed through the power of His Word and the Holy Spirit, in this place called New Hope Centre on Bethany Mountain in Swaziland, Africa.

God's Word says:

> *No eye has seen,*
> *no ear has heard,*
> *no mind has conceived*
> *what God has prepared for those who love him*
> *but God has revealed it to us*
> *By his Spirit.*
>
> —1 Corinthians 2:9–10 KJV

We can now look back and say, "Little is much when God is in it." We now have a mountaintop that reveals God's love and power. This mountaintop is covered with buildings and children with happy faces and joyful hearts. We hear the sound of laughter of children playing and singing praises to God. There are many little children at New Hope Centre who will be the leaders of tomorrow—orphans today, but leaders tomorrow. They are ensigns on the mountain that God will one day raise up. Then the world will see and know that this work all started when a little child began to lead our hearts into the heartbeat of God.

June's message was, and is, this: "When we look into the eyes of these children, we hear the heartbeat of God. No natural eyes saw this place. No natural ears heard this joyful sound of the children. God revealed His plan to me by His spirit, and somehow, someway, you, Elizabeth, caught the vision. It is a vision that will live on within the Swazi nation. The children of New Hope Centre will one day stand up and call both of us blessed, for we have done all we can to be Proverbs 31 women within the nation of Swaziland. Our Heavenly Father has an ensign on Bethany Mountain, where one day a mighty spiritual army will spring forth. The army is now in training. That is why they have joyful hearts and happy faces. They know their God, and they will be strong and do exploits.

"The prophet Joel also saw this army. He said, "They shall run like mighty men; they shall climb the wall like men of war; and they shall march every one on his ways, and they shall not break their ranks" (Joel 2:7). We are waiting for that day."

June was to have an audience with the King again, for which we had to wait. When at last she did have audience with the King, she raised the matter of the coming flood of orphans to Swaziland due to the challenge of HIV. His Majesty arranged to give June land to build the first children's home to start the work of caring for bereft children in the nation.

June returned with her board, End-Time Harvesters for the Nations, in December of 1998 to check out the land the King had given her. She returned with plans from an American master builder. While she was in Swaziland, her board said that the land was not suitable for a children's home, as it was too far from stores, supplies, clinics, and hospitals to be appropriate, although it was in a beautiful location in the hills.

The decision was made that they would instead search for a hotel or a place to purchase instead of building a centre. At that time, the Christian churches in the land had been successful in closing down many of the local hotels that were little more than dens of iniquity. Many of these hotels were for sale. We negotiated and nearly signed a deal on the Assegai Hotel in Hlatikhulu, the first capitol used by the British protectorate, located down in the hills in the south of Swaziland. This hotel had a major piece of land in the downtown area of the city, and was located across the street from the government hospital. The negotiations were in the final three weeks before settlement when the widow who owned the property died. Her sons decided that rather than selling it, they would try to run the hotel as their inheritance. So that deal was lost.

I got to know June first as a powerfully-anointed woman of God with a special knowledge and understanding that came from a deep and broad relationship with God. She is an amazing prophetic teacher, and brings the heart of God to each and every gathering. At the end of her two-week December trip, when she had been teaching much on the coming revival in Swaziland, and just as she was leaving at the airport, I asked if she would consider being the international speaker for the Somhlolo Festival of Praise in July. She agreed. I then confirmed it with Pastor Zakes Nxumalo. Afterward, I proceeded to the National Committee of the Festival and recommended her as the speaker. So in July of 1999, she returned as international speaker for the Somhlolo Festival of Praise with the theme "Arise and Shine in Ninety-Nine."

We started the two-week festival by chartering a flight to anoint the borders of the country with oil. There are times when God does unusual miracles to capture the attention of those to whom He wants to speak. Sometimes the lame walk; sometimes the blind see; sometimes manna falls from heaven to feed the hungry. God is not limited by our ideas of what will accomplish His purposes. He is only interested that He can accomplish the work He wants to do.

When June came to Swaziland, God performed an amazing miracle that has been repeated a few times in the last ten years. So while this miracle is amazing, and you may never have seen it or heard of it before, God certainly used it to capture the attention of those who long to see Swaziland redeemed by God. This is what happened:

I was the national co-coordinator of the festival that year, and was awakened early by the Lord to go and check the convention centre where the breakfast was to be held. This breakfast included diplomats, government leadership, church and business leadership in the country, the Prime Minister, and June, the international speaker of the Festival. The *Emakhosikati* (King Mswati III's young wives or queens) usually attend the breakfast, and the King sends a representative to grace the breakfast and speak on behalf of His Majesty.

I arrived at about 6 A.M., as the staff was starting to set up. There was glitter or gold dust everywhere. I asked if there had been a party the night before. The staff said no. I instructed them to repeat the vacuuming and clean it all up, as I did not want any suggestion that we had faked it. When I returned a few hours later just as the guests were arriving, we found the entire place was once again covered with sprinklings of cornflake-sized, sparkling gold dust. One of the senators warned the Prime Minister, saying, "When you enter the hall, do not be surprised to see gold dust the size of cornflakes all over everything. It is a strange phenomenon that follows the international speaker, Dr. June McKinney."

I am a scientist, and I will acknowledge that the mysterious appearance of gold dust cannot be explained by anything man knows. It amazed me along with everyone else to find gold dust in the scrambled eggs, under the table, on the tables, in people's hair, and even to find tiny gold particles on our faces. We just know that on this occasion, God wanted to communicate His desire for Swaziland to be joined to Him as a bride is joined to her husband. You may be wondering what happened to the gold dust after its appearance. Like the manna in the Old Testament, after a while, it disappeared.

These were the exciting days of coming to know this mighty woman of God. In May 2000, she returned, and we held an amazing national conference in the National Church—a four-day event with many signs and wonders. Her theme for the conference was "Fear not, O Swaziland." Her theme scripture was Joel 2:11, which says, *And the LORD shall utter his voice before his army: for his camp is very great: for he is strong that executeth his word: for the day of the LORD is great and very terrible; and who can abide it.* Even though Swaziland was facing sheer devastation from AIDS, believers were to hope and not fear.

Several years later, the international speaker of the Somhlolo Festival of Praise was a young Xhosa man, Pastor Tswana. He preached a message on God's purposed will for men and women. He spoke that we were created to have dominion over all the earth and every living thing. He showed that as male or female, we are biological beings responding to our chemical and hormonal composition. Second, as man and woman we are created differently; the man with strength to work and to provide sustenance and safety for the woman, the woman to nurture and care for the man to whom she is a helpmate. Third, we are mothers and fathers to serve our children and families: one as nurturer and comforter, the other as provider and security. Finally, the climax of our purpose and calling in life is to be an Abraham, father to the nations, or a Deborah, mother to the nations. After the event, God gave me a revelation with regard to the role of women in His kingdom. Of particular importance was a sermon about Deborah, found in the Book of Judges.

Deborah was a prophetess and the wife of Lappidoth. She was the judge who led Israel at that time. She held court under the Palm of Deborah in the hill country of Ephraim. The Israelites would come to her to have their disputes decided. Her story is in Judges 4:4–9. One day, *"She sent for Barak son of Abinoam from Kedesh in Naphtali and said to him, "The LORD, the God of Israel, commands you: 'Go, take with you ten thousand men of Naphtali and Zebulun and lead the way to Mount Tabor.'"* God was going to lure Sisera, the commander of Jabin's army, with his chariots and his troops to the Kishon River and deliver him into Barak's hands.

Barak said to her, *"If you go with me, I will go; but if you don't go with me, I won't go."*

"Very well," Deborah said, *"I will go with you. But because of the way you are going about this, the honor will not be yours, for the LORD will hand Sisera over to a woman."*

And God did deliver the evil Sisera into the hands of a woman (see Judg. 4:17–21). Then Deborah and Barak sang a song, and in one verse of the song they sang, *"Village life in Israel ceased, ceased until I, Deborah, arose, arose **a mother in Israel"*** (Judg. 5:7, emphasis mine).

A "mother in Israel"? What was a "mother in Israel—a mother of a nation"? What did she do? How was she different from other women? The words "mother of a nation" gripped my soul.

The sermon was about God's heart concerning women. This was a highly unusual topic in Africa, where women don't have much honor or recognition. What I saw was not surface—just the treatment of women—it went much deeper. It went to the core of who we are as women. It was about God's plan for women. Some women were mothers and some were Deborahs. And Deborah was a mother to a nation. Being female related to our biology. Being women related to our social stage. And being mothers related to our nurturing role. But Deborah was not only a mother; she was a mother to a nation—a mother to a nation granted the responsibility for the protection, survival, and prosperity of a multitude of people without hope if she failed to step into her calling.

Pastor Tswana's message troubled me. He said that every nation needed a Deborah. As a single woman, I could identify with being female and being a woman, but the mothering part? I had fostered several children for brief periods of time over the years, and I had been a spiritual mother to many. But a mother to a nation as I felt God was speaking to me?

As a young girl, I had read in 1 Corinthians 7:8, *"Now to the unmarried and the widows I say: It is good for them to stay unmarried, as I am. But if they cannot control themselves, they should marry, for it is better to marry than to burn with passion,"* and, *"An unmarried woman or virgin is concerned about the Lord's affairs: Her aim is to be devoted to the Lord in both body and spirit. But a married woman is concerned about the affairs of this world—how she can please her husband. I am saying this for your own good, not to restrict you, but that you may live in a right way in undivided devotion to the Lord"* (1 Cor. 7:34–35).

When I had read that, I had asked God for the grace to live life as a single woman, believing it was the way to be most effective in the Kingdom of God. A woman who is a spouse cannot help but be entangled with the requirements of that position; and somehow, even as a child, I knew that my life was going to be adventurous and that there would be many adversities. This was not going to be a life conducive to being a mother . . . or so I thought. This message gripped my being, and I knew that God was drawing me into His understanding.

I decided to take a week for prayer and fasting. On the fourth day of the fast, the Lord not only spoke to me, but He downloaded His vision and His desire for the children of Swaziland. He spoke to me about taking on the role of a Deborah—a mother in Swaziland.

In that moment, I felt like Noah, as God laid out a beautiful vision before me. I saw a house—right down to its exact dimensions, measurements, and rooms. I scribbled it all down. The house faintly resembled an ark, because it was built entirely of wood. Wooden homes are not often built in Swaziland, because of problems with termites and the climate. But that was what I saw—a wooden house. I could even see the children in the house, and as I looked, I began to understand that what God was showing me was a family. Not a typical family of father, mother, and children, but a family comprised of the castoffs and rejects of society. There were children, widows, young women, and young men. These were the most destitute of the destitute. I could see house parents, young women and men who would tend the grounds and act as aunts and uncles to the children. I saw the children, dancing and playing. Here, these outcasts of society would not only find their home, as the Word says, God *setteth the solitary in families* (Ps. 68:6), but these young ones would become leaders of tomorrow.

As I continued to look, I learned that this wasn't just a home. There was a school and a preschool on the grounds. God showed me that He wanted these orphans not only to have a home, but a place where they could be embedded in the Word of God and engulfed by it. He said He wanted to surround these children and fill them with Himself. There would be a Tabernacle of Praise on the mountain, where the praise of these children would ring out to silence the avenger—the avenger being death, AIDS, sickness, destruction, hopelessness, and despair. Then to my mind came the words of Psalm 8:2: *Out of the mouth of babes you have ordained praise.* And in this place—this mountain—they would sing and dance and make music with timbrels, drums, and instruments. They would play "on the harp, the lyre, and the tambourine." This would be a place of joy and praise on the mountain.

In Habakkuk 2:2 (NKJV), the Lord says, *Write the vision, and make it plain on tablets, that he may run who reads it.* I needed to be ready to share it with others and be ready to move forward. I was full of joy and excitement, but it was such a big vision. Noah built an ark in the time of a flood and saved a generation. This home was to be an ark in a flood of death, disease, and despair, in order to save a nation.

Not long after this vision, I was in South Africa with June, when along the highway we saw a house very similar to the one I had seen in my vision. It was wooden, a rare feature in Sub-Saharan Africa. This was the house—the exact reality of the house I had seen. We took a picture of it and went to the community to find out who had built it. We discovered that it had been built by a timber company in Nelspruit, up near Kruger National Park. We went to them, and the first thing the builders asked was what our budget was. Budget? We had no budget, so we told them we didn't know. The truth was that we didn't have *any* money at the time. Despite that fact, we asked them to draw up plans and give us a quotation of what it would cost to build the house I had seen in my vision. Then we would begin to pray for funds.

Living by faith was something I was used to as part of a missionary family. I had learned that when God gives you a vision, He also gives you the faith to see it done, and He gives you the people to make it happen. So June and I went to the Ministry of Justice in Mbabane, the capital of Swaziland, and registered the name of the organization as a non-profit, section 21 organization called New Hope Centre. This was to be a home for abandoned, orphaned, destitute children. We didn't have the home yet, but we had the hope that this great vision would come to pass.

Next, with the help of the Christian Media Centre in Manzini, we got the word out about New Hope Centre. They helped us make a video of the drastic developments of HIV/AIDS in lives in Swaziland. We also talked of a possible site—one which we could negotiate with the local community chiefs. I also printed a pamphlet outlining the vision (see appendix). On the evening of the very day I picked up the pamphlets from the printer, the pastor from my neighborhood came to my house. He told me he had been fasting and praying for three days and the Lord had spoken to him about fifty-seven acres of mission land in his charge. God had told him to use the land for the care of orphans. God said that He had shown me how to care for them.

I was amazed, and handed him the pamphlet. The ink was barely dry. I told him to read it, and if my vision given in the pamphlet lined up with his, then I would certainly know what to do with the land. The pastor went to his church committee, and the proposal for us to get the land began working its way up through proper channels. Soon, the Africa Evangelical Church approved the land use and in trust gave us fifty-seven acres to develop New Hope Centre and the ministry to orphans that was to impact the entire nation. I had just become a "mother to a nation."

We had the land, but now we needed money to start building. The only resource we had in abundance was prayer, and six copies of the video and a thousand pamphlets. I mailed the pamphlets to everyone I knew, and the six videos went to a few friends to tell them what was on the heart of God. Then we prayed and watched for God to provide.

Far off in Kelowna, British Columbia, Canada, Stephanie Mallens, a lab technician and member of the Hope for the Nations board, received an e-mail from Swaziland, and she was amazed. For the last year, AIDS had been her focus of research as a lab technician. As she did research, again and again the nation of Swaziland would come up on her computer screen as a place that AIDS was devastating. She began to be troubled, and then burdened, by the statistics she was seeing, and she began praying for this tiny African nation. God was giving her the heart and opportunity to play a role in rescuing it from the grip of death.

It is a small world. One of the videos I sent went to Carla, a missionary friend in Thailand. She watched the video, then went to her friend who had an orphanage and asked her how she had been able to start. The friend told her about a ministry called Hope for the Nations. This was a ministry dedicated solely to orphans and vulnerable children. They built homes for abandoned and destitute children around the world. To make a long story short, in February 2003, June and I were on a flight to Kelowna to meet Stephanie and the Hope for the Nations board to share our vision. They quickly understood that we were committed to caring for orphans and making leaders for tomorrow. This matched their commitment: "Orphans today . . . Leaders tomorrow." In May, a team was sent to Swaziland from their ministry to inspect the area. After four days, President Ralph Bromley told us that they had the money to build the home. Our hearts overflowed with praise and gratitude to our God, who leads us surely toward the calling He has placed in our hearts.

In June, 2003, the timber company from Nelspruit came to Swaziland. We recruited some men from the community to start digging the foundations of our house. And then, while the house was nowhere near finished, on July 26, 2003, we had a dedication service. Members of the Royal Family, UNICEF, churches, and, of course, June McKinney came stomping through the dust to bless this land and what it would become—just as my grandparents had done on another grassy hilltop when they first arrived in Swaziland. Our patron, Queen Lamagwaza, gave the King's speech.

The actual opening of New Hope Centre was a little less than a year later, in March 27, 2004, and while it had been very dusty at the dedication in July 2003, when the actual day of opening came we had a downpour of rain. It was so bad that the road had to be graded that morning so cars could come up the hill. We had to cover the ground with plastic sheets so people could walk on top of the mud and puddles. By this time, we had a steel frame and the roof of the tabernacle in place, but there was no foundation and no concrete floor. The floor was a clay mud bath.

Even though the rain and the mud were inconvenient, we were grateful for the rain. It is a Swazi belief that any event blessed with an abundance of rain is a sign of God's pleasure and announces His blessing on an event. So we praised God as the heavens burst open and baptized New Hope Centre at its dedication with an abundance of rain and with God's favor.

We did not know until the official opening, in March, when the speech of King Mswati III was read by one of his brothers, that this mountain was truly majestic. We learned then that this was the place where King Somhlolo had grown up, and where he had herded his father's goats and cattle. It was also the place where he had received the visitation from God that would change the course of his life and the life of his nation. Outside of God's grace and goodness, it was unthinkable that the very land where King Somhlolo had his vision would now house New Hope Centre—a place where we expected God to meet us once more.

As New Hope Centre director, I was commissioned by King Mswati III to raise the children who would come to this place to hear the voice of God, so that they could see Him just as King Somhlolo had done. It was as though the King of Swaziland was instructing me to do the very thing that God had put on my heart to do.

After the King's speech was read, June stood to give her blessing on New Hope Centre. As its spiritual founder, she would not just bless the foundations, but she would play a pivotal role in the life of each child who would one day call this place home. As she prayed, she began to prophesy about the future of our new arrivals. Her words only heightened our growing anticipation for the arrival of our orphans. These would be God's chosen ones. Our first three children had arrived on September 1, 2003. By the time of the opening, we had eleven precious, beautiful children. They sang together Dottie Rambo's classic, "Jesus, I Heard You Had a Big House."

Jesus, I Heard You Had a Big House

Jesus, I heard you had a big house
Where I could have a room of my own
And Jesus, I heard you had a big yard
Big enough to let a kid roam
I heard you had clothes in your wardrobe
Just the right size that I wear
And Jesus, I heard if I give you my heart
Then You'd let me go there.

Jesus, I heard about meal time
When all your children come to eat
I heard you had a great big table
Where every kid could have his own seat
Jesus, they said that there'd be plenty
Of good things in Heaven to share
And Jesus, I'd just love to tell you
I sure would love to go there

Jesus, I heard in your big house
There's plenty of love to go around
I heard there's always singing
And laughter to fill the place with happy sounds
And I've been thinking that a friend
Who'd planned to give me all that He's got
Before I even had met Him
Well, He sure must love me a lot
And Jesus, I just want to tell You
Well, I sure do love you a lot

—Bill and Gloria Gaither
(Used by permission)

**Speech by HIS MAJESTY KING MSWATI III
At the official opening of NEW HOPE CENTRE
AT NOKWANE**
On 27 March 2004

EMASKHOSIKATI
YOUR ROYAL HIGHNESSES
PRIME MINISTER
VENERABLE CHIEFS
COUNCILLORS
CABINET MINISTERS
EXCELLENCIES MEMBERS OF THE DIPLOMATIC
CORPS
MEMBERS OF BOTH HOUSES OF PARLIAMENT
REV. DR. JUNE MCKINNEY
DISTINGUISHED GUESTS
LADIES AND GENTLEMEN

INTRODUCTION

I greet you all at the New Hope Centre, here at Nokwane.

I am delighted to join you at this very important ceremony to mark the official opening of the New Hope Centre here at Nokwane.

The establishment of the New Hope Centre could not have come at a more opportune time, when the Swazi nation is facing the consequences of the killer HIV/AIDS scourge.

The nation is doing everything possible to mitigate the impact of the pandemic, as it breaks the social fabric of our society by destroying the family unit, thereby exposing children to poverty, abuse, trauma, and frustration.

It is disturbing indeed to note that the number of home-steads that are headed by very young children is increasing every day. These orphans go through traumatic moments as they had to care for their ailing parents before they buried them. Quite often, these young children have to drop out of school, as they have to fend for a living for themselves and for their younger brothers and sisters.

It is indeed very unfortunate that our traditional family care system might now be a thing of the past, as it surrenders to the battering of economic hardships and the introduction of other cultures that emphasize the concept of a nuclear family unit.

It is therefore imperative that our communities, and the entire Swazi nation, should find new systems of caring for our destitute children.

New Hope Centre

It is for that reason that, as a nation, we welcome the estab-lishment of this New Hope Centre with warm arms.

The establishment of this centre is in line with what the government is advocating, through NERCHA and other agencies, whereby we call on all communities to care for those who have been affected by the pandemic, in particular the orphans and the vulnerable children.

It is pleasing to learn that this centre will provide both shelter and schooling, based on biblical principles, for the inhabitants.

It is neither a coincidence nor a mistake that such a centre has been built on Mount Nokwane. This is indeed the providence of the Almighty God, Jehovah Jirah, our provider.

Let me remind the nation that Mount Nokwane was the home of none other than King Somhlolo, who had the ear of God. It was to King Somhlolo that God revealed that the Swazi nation shall prosper and succeed only if we choose to walk in the precincts of the Lord's eternal Word.

All the children who shall be fortunate enough to be accommodated at this centre shall be blessed indeed, as they shall dwell on the mountain where once dwelleth the noble King who was able to distinguish the voice of the Almighty God, provided, of course, that they emulate our King Somhlolo.

Foundation and Sponsorship

It befits this moment that we should turn our attention to the visionary, prophetess, and servant of God. This is none other than Rev. Dr. June McKinney, whose holy ear is as sharp as that of King Somhlolo.

It is through her obedience to God that we are today gathered here to witness this momentous occasion.

When she first came to share her vision with me in 1998, I thought, well, maybe she might be just one of those who sees visions and just carry on seeing more. But thank God, she is unique, outstanding, and a woman of action who deserves our warmest hands of applause. We thank God for you, Dr. McKinney. May He continue to bless you abundantly.

It is most encouraging to note that this centre has been built with funds pouring from loving hearts from many countries all over the world. We say thank you to all those who have responded to God's call for such a noble cause.

Last, but not the least, we recognize with pride the contribution that has been made by our own Dr. Elizabeth Hynd and the many other local sponsors in the establishment of this centre.

Conclusion

In concluding my remarks, let me assure the New Hope Centre that the government and the entire Swazi nation will continue to support your good work. We encourage other organizations and communities to emulate your contribution to the national fight against the HIV/AIDS pandemic.

It is government policy that such centres should be built in every community. We sincerely believe and pray that orphans should be accommodated within their own familiar environment so that they do not lose their identities and break roots from their folk.

We are convinced that such arrangements will enable them to heal faster from their trauma, so that they may grow up like all other children.

We encourage the New Hope Centre to work closer with NERCHA and other organizations, so as to enhance the coordination of our national programs.

Again, thank you to all persons and organizations that have made this noble mission the success that it is. Let us all continue the fight for the preservation of the Swazi nation, as we look forward to an AIDS-free era, which we shall reach through the grace of the Almighty God.

Declaration

It now gives me the greatest pleasure to declare the New Hope Centre at Nokwane officially open.

Thank you. May the Almighty God Jehovah bless us all.

New Hope Centre Opening Speech
by Rev. Dr. June McKinney
Mother and Prophet to the Nation

March 27, 2004

Bethany Mountain, near Manzini, Swaziland

Praise the Lord! How wonderful it is to be back home in Swaziland. Before I go into what the Lord has given me to share this morning, I ask each one of you to put your arms around yourself like this and receive a hug from me to you.

Prince . . . representative of His Majesty King Mswati III, we are blessed to have your presence.

Your Excellency Prime Minister Themba Dlamini, I have prayed for you since you came into office.

My good friend Prince Masitsela, Manzini Regional Administrator, I bless you to live a long life.

To the Royal Family, my friends, and my mother Princess Msalela.

To my good friend Ben Nsibandze, Hhohho Regional Administrator, and your family.

Pastor Zakes, it has been a long time since we have been around Swaziland together and traveled around America together. It is good to see you.

Dr. Babe (Papa) Hynd, blessings, and may you live a long life. And when you do go, may you go from the Manzini Medical Clinic, though I can't imagine a Swaziland without Babe Hynd.

Greetings and blessings to you all, Babe Shongwe, Minister of Works. Thank you for your help and the use of your talents to liaise with His Majesty on behalf of New Hope Centre.

Please stand for one more prayer. Let us bow our heads before the throne of heaven and talk with the King of Glory.

Mighty God that you are, we thank you that we can come and stand on this hallowed land. We thank you that you have geographical boundaries in heaven that meet earth, and that you sanction and anoint a land and a work. Lord, we thank you for the ministry of angels that surround us. Thank you that the Kingdom of Heaven, which we cannot see, is more real than the world we live in. We acknowledge this kingdom today in Jesus' name. We say, "Come, Holy Spirit, in your power and your wisdom, and impart this vision in the life of the children and all who are under the sound of my voice." From this mountain raise up a mighty ensign, O Lord—a place where the cripple will be healed and where the hungry will be fed. Though famine may strike again, Lord, you said the righteous need not worry, for you would always take care of them. Lord, we ask that you would mark this place in this nation. Father, we ask that you would bring the Body of Christ completely together so that we can share the visions that we have in common and so that we can stay focused and all be going in the same direction.

Lord, I thank you for this nation. We lift up Their Majesties in Jesus' name and we say, "Father, bless them and bless this land." Lord, take this word and serve it to us in the spirit realm as you did with the five loaves and two fishes, so that we will leave with more understanding as to why you erected this house, and why you selected a Home of Happy Overcomers here. Father, we thank you for the blood that covers. I bring into captivity every thought to the obedience of Christ Jesus. Thank you, Father, for the Word that you have for us today, and thank you for the leaders of tomorrow who will come out from this home. In Jesus' name, Amen!

A *vision* is God allowing someone to see into His plans and His heart for a certain need. When someone sees a vision, then God can create His plan. At that time, others can see what only one person saw in the beginning. When Moses was selected to be leader of Israel to lead God's people out of bondage as a nation, God had heard a cry. Though Moses was on the backside of the desert, the children of Israel were crying in Egypt. God responds to a cry, and God has heard the innocent cry of children from the womb of mothers in this nation. God has erected this home—New Hope Centre—for one purpose: to show His glory. We believe that from this home, future Christian leaders will be raised up in Swaziland. We believe that someday, a trained swimmer from this home will be on an Olympic team and will bring back to Swaziland a gold medal from this place. We believe that future musicians, dancers, and singers will come from this place. We believe that future prophets, priests, apostles, and pastors will come from this place. God can do that. We look into the unseen and draw out what God has already seen. When we capture a vision and bring it into existence, everybody else sees it as well.

I want to read to you from Psalm 72:2–4. In America many years ago, we experienced our teenagers falling in love with death. Many of them hung themselves. The enemy tried to wipe out a future generation, but he could not. In Swaziland we are experiencing a curse, and before we go on, I want you to look down at your body. We are going to make a proclamation. The reason I am having you make this proclamation is this. In 1989, when I came into Swaziland for the very first time, the Lord spoke a scripture to me. I fell in love with this land, and I love it more every time I come to Swaziland. I believe the Word of God, and I believe the Word spoken in season will cause the Holy Spirit to take that Word and cause it to take root. I have cut out of my Bible the Word of God in Isaiah 60:22 that says, *A little one shall become a thousand, and a small one a strong nation: I the LORD will hasten it in his time.* His time. You are not dead. You are still alive, so look down at your body and say, "I have the strength of a thousand." You have the strength of a thousand, and this small nation will become a strong nation. One day AIDS will cease to exist in Swaziland. God will do it in His time. You can see that you are not dead. You do not have AIDS, but even if you do, you can get our book called *Eat the Word and Live*. It will give you scriptures and truth about God's healing power.

God has a promise and destiny for this land, and because He does, Satan has sent out a curse that he will wipe out this nation. The enemy wants to wipe out the nation of Swaziland. Here at New Hope Centre, we want to take the children of parents who have died, and we want to raise them up to be Olympic winners, teachers, preachers, prophets, apostles, musicians, singers, and dancers. Because we want to do that, I want to share with you what God wants to do. Let every man be a liar, but let God speak truth—His word is true. I want to share from Psalm 72:2–4.

He [God] shall judge thy people with righteousness, and thy poor with judgment. . . .

Listen to what He says:

He shall judge the poor of the people, he shall save the children of the needy, and shall break in pieces the oppressor.

How can God do that in this nation? It starts with the church. We the church begin to speak God's Word. We begin to proclaim God's Word. We speak a positive for every negative. The Word of God says, *Why should I die before my time?* (Eccles. 7:17). When I see the reports on the Internet and in the news media about Swaziland, the reports do not give you good coverage. They do not give America good coverage, either. They are paid to give a negative report, so I believe the negative is going out around the world about Swaziland so as to make the world aware that there is a Swaziland. One day, in God's timing, all of a sudden you Swazis will get up out of bed and will have the strength of a thousand, and this small nation will become a strong nation, and our children, called the "Abraham Kids," will be prophesying from this mountaintop. They will be reading from God's Word; they will be dancing all over the mountain. God has ordained a visitation for this nation; please hear what the Spirit of the Lord is saying. If I was the devil (and I am not), I would try to wipe Swaziland out, because God has ordained and destined a revival, an outpouring, a refreshing on this nation that no other nation has ever known. It is going to happen. This is the pulpit God is going to use to make known His works, and when it happens, the news media will hear of strange phenomena taking place in this nation. They will come from the north and the south, from the east and the west, and they will taste and see the goodness of the Lord.

I live and breathe and eat and sleep and speak this end-time revival that God will bring. So be not discouraged. Take courage. You are well able to possess this land; you are able to be the satellite for the power of the Holy Spirit. I believe the media is working for us in setting the stage.

The Bible says that children are the heritage of the Lord. These little ones God has sent to us—we make sure we hug each one a hundred times a day. It is very important that the children be hugged many times a day so they feel the touch of love, and so they feel and know Christian affection. We speak the Word of God over these children. If one of them is not resting at night, one of the caregivers or a staff member will come and sit with them and pray with them, comforting them until they are peaceful and feel loved and safe. This is the heritage of the Lord. Children are special. The Bible tells us they are the only people on earth who have angels—ministering spirits who ascend and descend continuously to the face of the Father. I have no children in the natural. I tell people Swaziland is my child. We do not take this ministry lightly.

Before I close, I want to read Zephaniah 3:19 (KJV). Remember, I told you that God in His destiny has a time when He will visit Swaziland with revival, with fire, with power, and with the Holy Ghost. When that happens, this is what the Bible says will happen.

Behold, at that time I will undo all that afflict thee: and I will save her that halteth, and gather her that was driven out; and I will get them [Swaziland] *praise and fame in every land where they have been put to shame.*

At that time will I bring you again, even in the time that I gather you: for I will make you [Swaziland] *a name and a praise among all people of the earth, when I turn back your captivity before your eyes, saith the LORD.*

God is not asleep. God is not mad at Swaziland. If anyone comes here condemning you while carrying God's Word, do not receive it. God loves this land. This is a land unlike any other land I have ever visited. It is set apart in destiny, and because of that, we need many workers here. We need many children. We need many grown-ups who have heard the call of God, and who respond to that call.

We have in our midst today Dr. Elizabeth Hynd. In the year 2000, the Lord sent her to my home in Jacksonville in a wheelchair. We stayed in my home and we ate the Word of God until her back was healed. I have seen her hunger for the Word of the Lord, and I know the lineage from which she comes. She comes from a godly heritage sent to this nation. To me, it would deprive the Swazis and cheat the Body of Christ if I did not set her aside today for the work of the ministry. My ministry is End-Time Harvesters for the Nations. My headquarters are in Jacksonville, Florida, but my heart is in Swaziland. I believe when I ordain someone for the ministry, I license that person for one year, and then we do an ordination.

I ask Dr. Elizabeth Hynd, Babe Dr. Samuel Hynd, Babe Rev. Alex Fakudze, and Make Flora representing Babe Absalom

Dlamini, Elizabeth's pastor, to come forward. We have her father in the natural. Please lay your hand upon your daughter and Make Flora, together with Pastor Absalom. Lord, watch over her soul. Please lay your hand upon her.

Elizabeth, we charge you in the mighty name of Jesus Christ of Nazareth to separate yourself from the cares of works and to enter into the hiding place under the wings of the cherubim and seraphim where the shadow of the Almighty dwells. I charge you in the mighty name of Jesus and under the anointing to speak the oracles of God, to separate yourself to seek His voice, to allow Him to break your heart again, to mold you and shape you and remake you to be a general in this end-time army. As all other generals gather, you will gather in their midst and you will march down the mountain and you will proclaim the oracles of God.

I speak to your spirit in the name of Jesus, and as the bridegroom in the Song of Solomon said, "Come away my Beloved, come away my Beloved and let us go, let us go once again and smell the roses and sit under the apple tree and let us come out where others will say 'who is this coming out of the wilderness leaning on the arm of the Beloved, coming out of the wilderness the desert place?'"

Thank you, Holy Father. In the company of Rev. Babe Zakes, Babe Dr. Hynd, and Make Flora and Babe Absalom, we license you for the work of the ministry, and in one year, we will ordain you publicly in the name of our Lord Jesus. Fight the good fight, Elizabeth. Press toward the mark of the high calling. Take up the mantle of your grandfather. Take the talents of your grandmother. Run with the wisdom of your father, and do that which God has called you to do in the mighty name of Jesus.

This is a hallowed spot on this mountain. This is a place God has preserved so you can see the children come forth. Just as the enemy tried to destroy Moses in the day God raised him up for the nation of Israel, we are sent here to salvage a remnant for God—to save the children who will save the nation. I would love to hug each and every one of you. I love you Swazis like none other on earth.

I am sharing at the Lobamba Christian Fellowship in the morning, then I leave on Monday. I will see you next time and maybe I can be translated here to you. That would be so much better than coming through customs. May the Lord bless you all. Amen!

Director Elizabeth Hynd's Message
At the New Hope Centre Opening

It is our privilege and joy to greet all of you at the New Hope Centre. This New Hope Centre is the first of its kind in Swaziland, as it is a permanent children's home for happy overcomers, a school for performing arts to teach us to praise and worship, a school of children's ministries, and a New Hope Centre farm filled with micro-projects.

In 1995, before we in Swaziland were even aware of the tragic events of the AIDS pandemic that was coming to visit the land, our Heavenly Father shared with His servant Rev. Dr. June McKinney that soon Swaziland would enter this affliction and we would have many orphaned children.

Rev. *"Make"* June McKinney began to pray concerning these matters, and in 1998, when His Majesty invited her as his special guest to the Thirtieth Independence Celebration, she had the opportunity to share with His Majesty what was on the heart of God concerning the children of this nation, and that she had a mandate from the Heavenly Father to build a home called the House of Edward. The name Edward means "Happy Overcomer" or "Happy Conqueror." These children have faced many challenges with the loss of family, loved ones, and their homes and relatives. They are truly challenged and equipped by God to become happy overcomers, as they must overcome with great strength and joy the challenges or mountains of circumstances that have been set before them.

His Majesty was touched by this mandate from heaven, and promised to assist Make June in any way he could to bring this about. Today we are opening this New Hope Centre, which is the beginning of the manifestation of what was on the heart of God. His Majesty has blessed the occasion, and blessed the work of God in this place.

In the meantime, I was living and working here in Swaziland, and God showed me in a vision while praying in my home here in Bethany that this mountain was a very special and sacred mountain, a mountain from which the nation of Swaziland was gathered into a sovereign nation. It is on this mountain that God has ordained a place of praise and rejoicing. He showed me that on this mountain, He would visit with His glory and His power. People who were crippled, sick, weak, and lame would be coming and be helped. Many would be helped to come up this mountain, where in the presence of the Lord they would receive healing, and return down the mountain leaping and dancing and praising God. It was very much like the story in Acts where Peter and John went into the temple and saw the crippled man. They told him, *"Silver and gold have I none but such as I have I give unto thee, in the name of Jesus Christ of Nazareth rise up and walk."* The man arose and not only walked, he went into the temple leaping and dancing and praising God. We serve a God who never changes. The power of God is still here to heal and restore, to bring life, joy, and strength, so that those who come to this mountain will experience the power of God. He showed me that there would be a Tabernacle of Praise from which joy and praise, dancing and leaping would take place; that the joy and strength of the Lord would be in this place, that miracles, signs, and wonders would be in this place, that there would be fields of food and fields of vineyards on this mountain.

In July of 2002, Pastor Tswana from Gauteng was one of the international speakers of Somhlolo Festival of Praise, and he preached a message that shook the very foundation of my soul and spirit. He spoke of the calling, the role, and the ministry of Deborah in the Bible. She was a woman of God, a judge in the land, a prophet in the land, and truly a mother of the nation that brought salvation and victory to Israel in their time of threat.

The Lord God called me into prayer to seek Him about this message and what was He saying to me. He was calling me to commit myself to enter and serve this nation as Deborah served her nation of Israel. Now this is very strange to me as I am not a mother of natural children, although I have been a mother to hundreds and thousands of spiritual children in the Kingdom of Heaven. I am not a judge by academic training, but I am a psychologist, scientist, a science educator, a business administrator, and a certified Supervisor and Developer in Educational Curriculum. God is a God of great wisdom. He has brought me through training in the biological and psychological sciences so that in this pandemic I have understanding. He has brought me through educational qualifications, that we may have a registered and successful school. He has brought me through business training, that we may have micro-projects to finance and support these homes and train these young people in farming, marketing, management, and business. He has also trained me on the job in evangelism, ministry in the teaching the Word of God, and the use of the gifts of the Holy Spirit to bring healing, restoration, revelation, and deliverance to those trapped by the enemy and his demons. God is a good God. I cannot go into the details of God's training and preparation, but today I stand before you assigned to serve this spiritual Israel as Deborah served the natural Israel in her times.

You may be asking the question as to how this is on land that our King gave once upon a time to missionaries from afar. The King saw that it was good before God to give land to the men and women of God, that they may be able to bring the blessings and revelations and prosperity of heaven down to the earth. As Christians and ministers of God, we are ordained to establish the Kingdom of Heaven on the earth, to replace the destruction and chaos of Satan and restore once more the joy and blessings of shalom. The Word of God tells us that the heart of the King is in the hand of God. So the heart of the King who gave this sacred land to the early missionaries was in the hand of God for that time and for this time.

By September, 2002, God had shown me what He wanted to do to bring about the visitation of His glory and miracles to this mountain: He wanted a children's home, for He has ordained praise in the mouths of children with power—you will see our scripture is found in Psalms 8:2. Today we are opening, with the blessing of the King of kings, and with the blessing of the King of Swaziland, this Likaya Lemaqhawe Lanenjabulo. Each child comes to this home to be adopted permanently, receiving a new name given from God out of the Bible that is prophetic over the child's life. Each child takes on the new surname Abraham, as we are the seed of Abraham, the father of faith. We have no building, no water, no food, no clothes except through prayer and faith that God is the Provider, God is our Source, as King Mswati III has stated on the money of our land. We have with us a servant of God who is called and ordained of God to serve the children in the nations of the Earth, to establish homes for orphans of today who will be leaders of tomorrow, *Babe* Ralph Bromley from Canada, president of Hope for the Nations. He is a partner that God has brought to serve with us, and he will greet you shortly.

Today, we are seated under the roof of the Tabernacle of Praise, which is to be the school of Performing and Fine Arts. We have with us another servant of God, *Babe* Izak Coetzee, who is the founder and president of Eden Ministries, who will be partnering with us as we prepare to present praise from this mountain in song, dance, worship, drama, and art—all to the glory of God in developing the talents God has invested in these children and in those within Swaziland who are hungry to worship God in spirit and in truth. There will be music and rejoicing coming from this place that will bring the glory of God. Like the icing on a cake, the glory of God will cover this mountain in the days to come. You will be blessed by the ministry of this man of God in worship and praise today; he is giving us a prophetic taste of heaven and of things to come on this mountain.

This year we have started two schools by God's grace. The preschool serves the orphans and the community, and you will be hearing from Miss Tracie, the head of the preschool, shortly. We have also launched the School of Tomorrow, which already has five students in primary school, and only yesterday, a man of God from South Africa came to register his three children in our school. This school is special, as it has a biblical curriculum. We have many Christian schools in Swaziland, but most follow the secular curriculum although the teachers and pupils are Christian. Our school is based on the Bible and the character traits of Jesus Christ of Nazareth. You will hear shortly from Miss Thandazile Ngwenya, the teacher of the School of Tomorrow.

You do not see with natural eyes today the home for teenage boys to come nor the home for teenage girls to come as these children will grow. This home you see today already has eleven children, and will become home to sixty children between the ages of 2 and 12. Then, as true Swazis, the teenage girls and the teenage boys will move into two new homes so that we will complete the number of one hundred twenty children, a full house as was found in the book of Acts on the day of Pentecost, when the Church was born by the visitation of the Holy Spirit with a mighty wind and tongues of fire.

You do not see in the natural eye the School of Children's Ministries, as God desires that parents, teachers, and children's workers throughout the country will need training to prepare the generation that will lead the continent of Africa in days to come, for the prophetic word in Isaiah 60:20–22 says the '*little one will become a mighty nation.*' The eye of the Lord God Jehovah is upon us, brothers and sisters in the nation of Swaziland.

You see the early beginnings of the micro-projects in the natural as you see our small vegetable garden. We hope the Lord will make a way for us to have a broiler chicken project, a weaving project, a project making lamb-skin slippers, and a project raising food and vegetables to export to the nations of Europe and the islands of the seas.

Today we are greatly blessed to have *Make* June McKinney with us, and she will be sharing the Word of God to the nation from this mountain today. We have *Babe* Ralph Bromley of Hope for the Nations, and Brother Pieter Colson, representing his father from the USA, to greet us. I will now ask our first international volunteer who has come to give his time, talents, love, and strength to New Hope Centre, followed by *Babe* Ralph Bromley, who has given his love, prayers, and provisions in multiplied portions to the New Hope Centre and to twenty nations around the world, to give us what is in his heart.

Now, we would like to introduce to you the family of New Hope Centre. *Make* Sarah will introduce Likhaya Lemaqhawe Lanenjabulo. Miss Tracie Hynd will introduce Sikholwa Semaqhawe Lanenjabulo Preschool, and Miss Thandazile Ngwenya will introduce the School of Tomorrow (Hope Academy), which is an Accelerated Christian Education School.

Chapter 4

SWAZILAND:
A BEAUTIFUL COUNTRY
WITH A PROFOUND
DESTINY

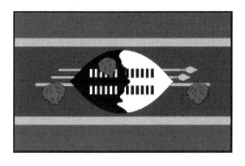

Like June McKinney, few people know much about
Swaziland. Where is it located? What is its history and
destiny? Part of the reason so little is known about our country
is that Swaziland has never been involved in a war. Wars and
bloodshed bring notoriety to countries through the media, but
this little land of less than one million people, established on
the vision of the founding King Somhlolo so many years ago,
is a land of peace and gentleness. Only recently has the media
found Swaziland and begun to make her known through a
tragedy of death, disease, and despair. Swaziland has one of the
highest HIV infection rates. I would like to introduce you to
more truth about this tiny mountain kingdom.

Swaziland is one of the smallest countries in Africa, and is a sub-Saharan landlocked country bordered by South Africa and Mozambique. The land is named after the Swazi people, a Bantu-speaking people who migrated southward over the centuries along the Indian Ocean coastline. Swaziland has a wide variety of landscapes, from the mountains along the Mozambican border to savannas in the east and coniferous forests in the north and west. Several rivers flow through the country, namely the Great Usuthu River and the White and Black Umbuluzi Rivers.

History

The Khoi-San people, the earliest inhabitants of this area, were *hunter-gatherers*, and their rock paintings are found in caves throughout the country. In the 4th century, there is evidence of agriculture and iron use, indicating that the people had already become farmers. By the 16th century, the Bantu peoples had migrated southward into what is now Mozambique. A few clans broke away from the main body in the 18th century and moved through the great southern gorge in the Ubombo mountain range to settle in Swaziland. In the 19th century, these clans became organized into a tribe, partly because of the warlike Zulu tribes to the south who threatened their existence through brilliant warrior-kings like Shaka Zulu. The Swazi leader, Mswati, appealed to the British in the 1840s for protection from the wars of Shaka Zulu. The British and the Transvaal governments guaranteed sovereign independence to Swaziland in 1881.

The Monarchy

As early as the 18th century, the ruling lineage had chiefs and chief-ships. It was King Sobhuza I who expanded the borders of Swaziland in the early 19th century. Soon the missionaries he sent for came, and other whites started to settle the area. In 1890, South Africa took sovereignty over Swaziland, but never established full power. After the Second Boer War (1899–1902), Swaziland became a British protectorate. Swaziland as it exists today is a young nation, having been granted independence by the British in 1968, ceding power to King Sobhuza II, a wise, gracious much-loved and honored King.

Swaziland's King Mswati III, who came to the throne in 1986, is sub-Saharan Africa's last absolute monarch. Tradition is that the King, the *Ingwenyama* (the Lion), as he is known, reigns alongside his mother or a ritual substitute who is called the *Ndlovukati* (She-Elephant). The King appoints a Prime Minister and some members of Parliament, while others are democratically elected (one person, one vote). The government is a Senate of thirty members and a House of Assembly with eighty-two seats. Political parties are banned, and the King can veto any law passed by the legislature. He frequently rules by decree.

Land Usage

Nearly sixty percent of Swazi territory is publicly held by the crown in trust of the Swazi nation. Despite the territories being held in trust by the crown, the land is still distributed to the people. The people are privileged to grow crops, make profit from selling their crops, graze livestock, and build either traditional or modern homes without paying any taxes to the government. Most of the private ownership of the remaining forty percent is by mixed Swazis, black Swazis, white Swazis, and foreign investors. Part of the remaining forty percent also includes the government and Tibiyo TakaNgwane, a company established by King Sobhuza II to be held in trust on behalf of the Swazi nation.

Swaziland has developed roads linking it with South Africa, and also railroads running east to west and north to south. The older east-west railroad link makes it possible to export goods from Swaziland through the Port of Maputo in Mozambique. A north-south rail link, completed in 1986, provides a connection between the Eastern Transvaal (now Mpumalanga) rail network and the South African ports of Richards Bay and Durban.

Sugar is one of the biggest industries of the country. It is Swaziland's leading export, along with soft drink concentrate. A large part of Swaziland's revenue comes from the Coca Cola Company, who, for tax reasons and easy access to vast amounts of cheap raw Swazi sugar, have located their concentrate plant in the country. The Coca Cola Company concentrate plant exports to a wide range of countries in Africa and elsewhere.

The country also exports wood pulp and lumber from cultivated pine forests, as well as pineapple, citrus fruit, and cotton. Swaziland mines coal and diamonds for export. There is also a quarry industry for domestic consumption. Recently, a number of industrial firms have located at the industrial estate at Matsapha, near Manzini, which is also near New Hope Centre. The fast-growing industrial sector at Matsapha produces garments, textiles, and a variety of light manufactured products. The Swaziland Industrial Development Company (SIDC) and the Swaziland Investment Promotion Authority (SIPA) have assisted in bringing many of these industries to the country. Government programs encourage Swazi entrepreneurs to run small and medium-sized firms, all of which are important to New Hope Centre's future. Tourism is also important to the economy of Swaziland, and attracts more than 424,000 visitors annually—mostly from Europe and South Africa.

Industry

For Swazis living in rural homesteads, the principal occupation is a combination of farming and livestock herding, and some have migrated to urban work or small-scale trades in either

Swaziland or South Africa. Cattle are important symbols of wealth and status.

Today, about seventy percent of Swazis live in rural areas that are periodically ravaged by drought, resulting in food crises that threaten hundreds of thousands with hunger and starvation. The unemployment rate is approximately forty percent, and nearly seventy percent of the population lives on less than one American dollar per day.

The People

The people of Swaziland have a gentleness and dignity that is unusual and unique in the continent of Africa. They have maintained peace with their neighboring nations of Zulus, Shangaans, Pedis, and Mndebeles through diplomacy and wisdom, and even with the colonial powers of the last two centuries. They have not known war or bloodshed, nor have they been oppressed or colonized. They have maintained sovereignty, respect, dignity, and humility. The advent of HIV/AIDS is a tragedy of death and degradation previously unknown to the Swazi nation.

Although the first recognized HIV diagnosis was in 1986, only in 2004 did Swaziland acknowledge that it was suffering an AIDS pandemic, with almost forty percent of the population infected, and ninety percent of the hospitals filled with patients dying of AIDS. Swaziland is recognized as having the lowest life expectancy (twenty-seven years) in the world—forty percent below average. Only ten years ago, life expectancy was sixty-seven years. The early demise of parents has left ten percent of the households in Swaziland headed by orphans. Not only is the country plagued by AIDS, but also by drought, land degradation, and increased poverty. The former United Nations special envoy on AIDS, Stephen Lewis, said, "Swaziland stands alone with the world's highest rate of HIV infection after nearby Botswana made headway against the deadly pandemic."

This is a nation in crisis—a dying nation. A nation that will be extinct by the year 2050, unless God intervenes.

The Future

Joel, a prophet in Bible, had a daunting task. Everywhere around him was destruction. There was no rain. An army of locusts had devoured, the few crops that had survived the drought, and Israel had once again turned its back on God. They were people filled with pain, who could see no hope on the horizon. Joel begins his book with this woeful message to the people:

> *Hear this, you elders;*
> *listen, all who live in the land.*
>
> *Has anything like this ever happened in your days*
> *or in the days of your forefathers?*
>
> *Tell it to your children,*
> *and let your children tell it to their children,*
> *and their children to the next generation.*
>
> —Joel 1:2–3

It is hard for most of us to imagine the kind of devastation Israel faced in that day, but we in Swaziland have an idea. Swaziland is in a situation that previous generations could not have imagined. While those who lived before might have had to contend with leprosy, typhoid, malaria, and the like, no one could have imagined the grip of death that has now come in like a flood on this generation. The dreams and destinies of a nation have been washed away prematurely. The sheer scope of the orphan crisis is unfathomable. The obituary pages of the newspapers are full of young faces—teachers, policemen, and laborers. All that are left are the young and the old. It is expected that at the time of writing that there are 200,000 orphans in this land with a population of 800,000.

The burden of the nation is huge, and much of it rests squarely on the shoulders of the grandmothers (*"gogos,"* as they are called). The load is often overwhelming, as they try to shelter a dozen or more grandchildren. At a time when their lives should be more peaceful and restful, they must become the breadwinners and disciplinarians for the family. Of course, there is no recourse but that the orphan children too must carry a tremendous load of responsibility for cooking, caring for younger children, caring for the sick and dying, and helping to bury the dead. Too often, these young ones receive little or no attention. They are starving for the love they need in order to develop into healthy, wholesome adults. It is tragedy upon tragedy for Swaziland's families.

But Joel was sent to deliver a message first of repentance and then of hope. He challenges Israel to mourn for their sins and to cry out to the Lord for mercy and forgiveness:

> *Declare a holy fast;*
> *call a sacred assembly.*
> *Summon the elders*
> *and all who live in the land*
> *to the house of the LORD your God,*
> *and cry out to the LORD.*
>
> —Joel 1:14

And he declares:

> *Return to me with all your hearts, with fasting, with weeping*
> *and with mourning.*
> *Rend your heart*
> *and not your garments.*

Return to the LORD your God,
for he is gracious and compassionate,
slow to anger and abounding in love,
and he relents from sending calamity.

—Joel 2:13

In the chaos and destruction all around him, Joel had a message of hope for Israel. If the nation would repent and return to God, he would deliver them from death and restore everything that has been lost. To the same degree that they were experiencing destruction on an unprecedented scale, they would one day also experience an outpouring of blessings beyond their dreams.

And afterward,
I will pour out my Spirit on all people.
Your sons and daughters will prophesy,
your old men will dream dreams,
your young men will see visions.

—Joel 2:28

In July 1999, June McKinney brought such a message to the nation of Swaziland while addressing tens of thousands at the National Thanksgiving Service during the Somhlolo Festival of Praise. Many use this scripture, but in Swaziland it is received with great hope and expectation. We believe we have already seen a glimpse of this promise beginning. Even though it appears that the AIDS pandemic in Swaziland is an overwhelming flood of death and despair, the Bible is filled with stories of God's intervention in conditions of suffering and despair. God always has a plan for His people. We believe that our little ones at New Hope Centre are part of God's plan as He is raising up a standard that will stop the flood.

When God showed me the vision for New Hope Centre, I didn't fully understand all that God had in His heart and mind. Only when, in obedience, we had built the big wooden home on the mountain did I begin to understand we are part of saving a generation, and in turn a part of saving a nation. God said that we were to seek out those who fell through all the social networks, the most destitute of children in Swaziland, and they would be transformed into future leaders of the country. These children are the standard raised up against the flood of disease, death, and despair. These are the leaders of tomorrow who will know the power and wisdom of God, and who will have His strength to stand for what is good, just, and true. The prophet Joel said that God would repay Israel for the years the locusts had eaten. And these children, sheltered here in our home, are the ones God will use to restore what the locusts have eaten in Swaziland and cause the faithfulness and goodness of God to be known.

One day, these little ones will have enterprises and businesses that will thrive, and the nation will be blessed with the proceeds from their endeavors. These children will not forget where they have come from, and how they were rescued and restored. With the same mercy they will rescue and restore others.

I have been in worship services where the ground literally shook with the praise of God's people, and I believe that a day is coming when the land of Swaziland will tremble with the sound of rejoicing as the people of Swaziland praise God for what He has done amongst us. Out of death and despair will come a rejoicing that will amaze, encourage, enlighten, and enliven all of Africa, and even extend beyond its shores.

A little one shall become a thousand,
And a small one a strong nation.
I, the LORD, will hasten it in its time.

—Isaiah 60:22 KJV

The Greater Glory

I thought working on this book would be a lot of fun, because I wanted to focus on God's greater glory. Jesus said he went to the cross and suffered ridicule, beatings, and even the rejection of His father. *About the ninth hour Jesus cried out in a loud voice, "Eloi, Eloi, lama sabachthani?"*—which means, *"My God, my God, why have you forsaken me?"* (Matt. 27:46). Jesus went to hell and came back and was resurrected, all because of the greater glory to be achieved at the end. You see, He had read the last page. He knew the end from the beginning.

But telling the story of New Hope Centre, and what we do, and why, has been difficult. Every time I tell the story of one of our children, my heart is torn, because as I tell even a tiny bit of their pain and suffering, I am so conscious that one of our children represents hundreds of thousands in Swaziland that are beyond our reach, not even "home alone," as they have no home. I do, however, see the greater glory that is ahead. Our children are not only the leaders of tomorrow, but of today. A leader is someone who can empower and influence others. Our children are already influencing the community in which we live, the church we attend, and the schools with which they are involved. They have already influenced others with hope because they are His hope manifested.

If my heart is broken by telling these stories, how much more is His heart broken? If I am aware of the need, how much more does He know the need? He who sees the sparrow fall sees the death and destruction, and the thousands of children who are left fatherless. It has never been His will for any of His children to be fatherless. *"A Father to the fatherless, a defender of widows, is God in his holy dwelling"* (Ps. 68:5). But God has a people who can hear and feel His heartbeat and His heartache while sensing the power of knowledge of faith, hope, and love. It is not His intent that they be oppressed and distressed, robbed of their home and security, their inheritance and land, as is happening across the country.

"Uncles" and "aunts" take advantage of their innocence, ignorance, dependence, and helplessness. Without a father, there is no security, no place in society, no one to stand for the rights and justice of a child. Even the bereaved widow is helpless in the culture, as she belongs to her husband's family, her brothers, and relatives. She may be there to give love and nurture for a while, but she too is helpless. As her health deteriorates, others begin making decisions on her behalf. The child is then vulnerable, lost, in distress, and often in despair. We can be part of His intervention—His standard raised up with strength, love, and hope. But to be part of the answer, we need first to receive His life, hope, and anointing.

Many times, wounded people—broken people—are among the first to volunteer to help our children, because they understand the pain and the need for comfort these children experience. So everyone who walks with our children on their journey of life helps to heal something in that child's life from where they too have been healed. Coming to walk with these children through their experiences provides the opportunity and privilege for each one of us to heal and move deeper into the hope of greater glory in our own lives, and in the lives of the children and the life of the nation.

You may wonder what I am talking about when I use the term "the greater glory," so let us go back to the prophet Joel. The prophet Joel continued in Chapter 2 to describe a glorious army, arrayed in splendor, marching in rank and order, the young and the old together. This army is confident in the Word of God, and confident in the will and purpose of God moving through the land.

They run like mighty men,
They climb the wall like men of war;
Everyone marches in formation,
And they do not break ranks.
They do not push one another;
Everyone marches in his own column.
Though they lunge between the weapons,
They are not cut down.
They run to and fro in the city,
They run on the wall;
They climb into the houses,
They enter at the windows like a thief,
The earth quakes before them,
The heavens tremble;
The sun and moon grow dark,
And the stars diminish their brightness.
The Lord gives voice before His army,
For His camp is very great;
For strong is the One who executes His Word.
For the day of the Lord is great and very terrible;
Who can endure it?

—Joel 2:7–11 NKJV

The day is coming when the children and the grannies (*gogos*) of Swaziland will come forth in this splendor, disciplined, confident, healthy, and strong. The knowledge of the Word of God they have learned to eat, the confidence of overcoming all the odds, all the despair and fear will be overcome by learning to trust the one and only wise God. This will be a day of wonder in the world. I have seen in the spirit realm the clans of Swaziland coming together on the plains of Lobamba, as the Israelites in their twelve tribes gathered together around the Tabernacle of God in the plains around Mount Sinai. The sound of praise and rejoicing will be heard over the mountains, even into the neighboring countries. The dust cloud of our dancing feet will be seen over the hills in Mozambique,

Mphumalanga, and Zululand. Even as today the young maidens gather each spring by the tens of thousands, so the young and the old will gather in the hundreds of thousands.

> *"Fear not, O land; be glad and rejoice: for the Lord will do great things."*
>
> —Joel 2:21 KJV

It is our deepest hope that this generation will deal with and overcome death and loss to this epidemic that is leaving behind thousands of orphaned children. We believe the scourge of AIDS will end before this generation passes. We know that the need for a children's home of the kind we have will only be for a season. This may be why we were to build a wooden house, rather than one made of concrete. God meant it to be temporary. A flood is a passing event, and this wooden house full of lively children is a standard raised against the flood of disease, death, and despair. The tide will be turned. Hope and laughter will be restored. And it will be the little ones—the despised and forgotten ones—who will take hold of the standard, and with arms raised high they will lead Swaziland into a new day of hope, peace, and joy. The Lord will *"give them beauty for ashes, the oil of joy for mourning, the garment of praise for the spirit of heaviness, that they might be called trees of righteousness, the planting of the Lord that He might be glorified"* (Isa. 61:3 NKJV).

PART II
ABRAHAM'S FAMILY

Chapter 5

LORD OF THE FLIES

My worst nightmare is found in the novel *Lord of the Flies*, written by William Golding and released during World War II. It is a disturbing story about a group of children evacuated from the UK and later shipwrecked on an island where they had no adult supervision. While waiting for a rescue that might never come, these children are left to their own devices. They have to find a way to survive and create a new life—a new order. Soon, they separate into two tribes with two leaders. They learn not only to survive, becoming master hunters and gatherers, but also to create a whole new society complete with a new religion of sacrifice. The boar becomes an important source of meat for them, and also an object of worship. But all is not well. A boy named Piggy is an outcast in this new society. Intelligent, but unable to hunt and kill, he is considered a weakling. He is heartlessly sacrificed by his peers.

This parable of the fallen nature of humans is disturbing. It is a nagging story of the potential for darkness that lurks in us all. "But *Lord of the Flies* is just a story," you might say. Not in Swaziland. Here, we're on the brink of this reality. There are droves of children being orphaned each day, and there is no one to watch over them. They are fending for themselves. I have seen numbers of homes with children eight, nine, or ten years old acting as heads of household. These children lose their childhood. They lose their opportunity to be educated. And on top of it all, they must care for the adults who are sick and dying. So what happens to the younger children in this scenario?

Tirzah

Tirzah was one of those marooned children caught in a situation she did not ask for and did not know how to escape. At eleven, she had never been to school, only to an orphan care centre, with "teachers" who did not even have a high school education and who had no training. Between the ages of eight and eleven, she had cared for thirteen family members, all of whom had died.

It began when her father returned from working in the mines in Johannesburg, where he had become infected with AIDS. He soon died. Her mother became infected with AIDS as well, and she died shortly afterward. Person by person, her family disappeared into the valley of death and never returned.

While AIDS comes swiftly and takes lives with speed, the phase between contracting the disease and dying from it is horrendous. It is hard to imagine a young child such as Tirzah spending all day washing bloody rags, cleaning up pus-filled sores, and washing away the other bodily fluids that ooze from AIDS victims. None of us can fully understand the loss this child felt as she washed those bloody handkerchiefs, knowing that just touching them could expose her to certain death. But this is what Tirzah did—thirteen times over. Since her family lived in a remote area of the country far from roads, there was no medical help available to her family, even if they could have afforded treatment. Much of Swaziland lives this way—cut off from medical care, education, and the wider world. During those three horrific years, not one social worker or community health worker came to visit this home.

Nothing stood between Tirzah and her younger sister and disease, forced labor, or illicit sex. Anyone who wanted the two of them could have taken them. When we found them, they were still living in their family's homestead with no one to protect them. Her story is not unique. In fact, you can multiply it by thousands of others, and you will begin to have an accurate picture of what the children of Swaziland are enduring. What's going to happen to these children? They may survive, but what kind of person comes out of such desperation and insecurity? What kind of new order will they create—something that looks like that of the children of *Lord of the Flies*? God help us!

Had it not been for a teacher and some missionaries who facilitated a feeding place where orphaned children could come for one meal a day, we might never have known about Tirzah, much less been able to rescue her. But we did find her and her sister. It took four hours of bumping along over dusty mountain tracks to collect them. Soon they were safe in their new home.

Although the conditions at New Hope Centre are far better than what the children had been experiencing—good food, a comfy bed, and clean clothing—the conditions do little to salve the wounds of their recent past experiences. Tirzah, like most of the children who come to live with us, was very withdrawn at first. We have to work with the children, talking to them and letting them talk. We pray and hug them to let them know they are safe. We hope they will soon begin to share their hurts and fears.

One Friday, as we were getting ready for our Sabbath meal, I could see that Tirzah was particularly sad. I asked her what was wrong. "I'm waiting to die," she answered. I began to probe a little deeper. "Everyone who has cared for sick people as I have, has died." She had seen that one day family members would be able to walk, work, and carry on with the business of living, and the next day they would be bedridden and sick, and never recover from their illnesses. And while Tirzah was alive and well, she was waiting for the other shoe to drop. She just knew she was next.

I took her by the hand and said, "How could it be that the God who loved you so much that He caused us to take two trips high into the mountains beyond the roads and into the tracks and hills to find you—how could that God abandon you to death now? Don't you think this God would have a plan for you? Would this God allow you to die after all that?" Tirzah said nothing. She just stared straight ahead. "No, Tirzah, this God has a plan for your life. He has rescued you out of all that sorrow you left behind. He has rescued you because he has a purpose for your life. He wants to take off your cloak of mourning and depression, and give you a new garment of praise and glory to put on. He's going to raise you with strength, joy, thanksgiving, and an understanding and knowledge of who He is."

I could see she was listening, but was still skeptical that what I was telling her could be true. I asked her, "Tirzah, can you believe even in the tiniest corner of your heart that what I am telling you is true?"

She began to cry and said, "Maybe."

"If you can just 'maybe' believe, we can ask the Holy Spirit to bring life to your 'maybe'." We prayed together, and she took the first baby step toward having hope in her life. By the help of the Holy Spirit, it was not to be her last.

Tirzah had to battle panic attacks of fear and despair. Every time she had a cough or a pain, she was sure she was going to die. We would pray for her and hug her and sing to her and allow the Holy Spirit to minister life to her. One night, she was tormented with the thought that she was about to die. As we started to pray for her, we realized demons had taken her over and were beginning to manifest. We commanded them in the name of Jesus to get out and be silenced. After two hours of retching and vomiting, Tirzah stopped being sick. Then she went to take a shower, and when she came out from the shower, she had a shining face. Tirzah's "maybe" had begun to grow, and it would soon grow into a confident "yes."

She has experienced a great deal of healing since she first came to us; an indication of how far she has come happened when I asked her what she would like to do when she grows up. With a shy, sparkly smile, she told me she wanted to be a nurse so that she can encourage and care for the little girls of Swaziland—little girls like her sister and herself. It is her desire to bring a life raft of hope and healing into the flood of death that washes over Swaziland.

Some months later, as her confidence and academic abilities developed, she joined the 10,000 point club in school. This means one hundred tests with a score of one hundred percent. She then boldly and confidently shared that she will be a medical doctor. While waiting on the Lord one Saturday morning, He talked with her about her future. Some weeks later, she waited on the Lord and He showed her the delight of her heart: a hospital run by herself in mountains of her home, called Calvary Hospital. She will make a huge impact in restoring health and hope to her nation.

Noah

This flood of death could have inundated Noah and his little brother Jesse, had their father not intervened to ensure that his sons would have a home when he could no longer provide one for them. Their mother had died three years before this time. Now their father, after having been in and out of the hospital for two years, was facing imminent death.

Nine-year-old Noah and six-year-old Jesse had been living on their own in Malkerns, a city not too far from New Hope Centre. Their home was a cube of corrugated metal and cardboard. There was no running water or sewers in their community, so they had to get water from the rivers and use a pit latrine toilet. These two little boys survived by drinking from a nearby river and eating one meal a day from the "Orphan and Vulnerable Children" (OVC) care point. They also ate grasshoppers after plucking off their legs and cooking them on the open fire.

One of the times their father was in the hospital, he heard about New Hope Centre on the radio. He contacted the police and asked them to bring us to see him at the hospital. He told us about his boys, and his heartbreak and concerns for their future. We then went to their home and brought the boys to live with us at New Hope Centre. One day I took the boys to visit their father. I asked him to explain to his sons why he wanted New Hope Centre to be their new home. It was heartbreaking to watch this man, frail with sickness, wrap his emaciated arms around his boys and tell them that this would probably be the last time they would ever see each other. As they sat under the jacaranda tree, with tears running down his face, he explained that this sickness had taken its toll, and there would be no cure for him. He had wanted to be there for them, to watch them grow, and to train them to be men, but he could not. So he had determined that the best place for them was at New Hope Centre. He knew we would raise them to know and trust God. He told them to listen and be good so that he could be proud of them. He even said he would buy them a TV and a bike, but he never got to fulfill that promise. Weeks later, he was dead, and his money went to pay his hospital bills. There was nothing left for his sons to inherit.

Even though their father left Jesse and Noah no earthly legacy, he had given them a rich inheritance of love and affection. And that love and affection has made all the difference in their lives. Today, they are two of our brightest children. Noah is an expert swimmer, dancer, and sportsman, and Jesse is a brilliant child, a worshipper who loves to play the drums, exuding joy and the liveliest of praise and worship.

Our children here at New Hope Centre have been rescued from the *Lord of the Flies* scenario, but there are thousands of children living this reality in Swaziland. One primary school we visited had three hundred fifty students, ninety percent of whom were orphaned. A large number of the children at the school have no one to feed them, so they have their meals there—if you can call them meals. Meals often consist of runny grits with bean soup on top. It isn't much, but it is better than nothing.

The teacher told us that the orphan children are the troublemakers. They are in the middle of every fight and bully situation, with a blatant disregard for rules and authority. Imagine this one school multiplied hundreds of times over in Swaziland. These children are not troublemakers by nature. They are like those little boys in the book; lost, shipwrecked on a lonely island, and stuck in the loss and grief process. They have no one to feed them and no one to give them personal, spiritual, and emotional attention, and because of this, they have little to give anyone else.

The Tribe of Despair

Just as there were two tribes in the *Lord of the Flies*, there are two tribes of orphans. One of these tribes has turned what has happened to them inward. They are depressed and in despair. They fail over and over in school because they are withdrawn and cannot manage their homework. They cannot read or write. They cannot concentrate.

One orphan, a twelve-year-old girl, was fortunate enough to have her school fees paid by a donor. But she lived far from school and had to catch a bus. That meant paying thirteen rand—two US dollars—each way. So she could only go a couple of times a week. By the time she got into school, she was already behind, and could never manage to catch up. She would fail and have to start the grade all over again. In the evenings after she returned from school, she was expected to work and make bread buns to sell in order to earn the bus fare she needed for school the next day. It was a recipe for disaster. There was no way she could ever succeed.

So why doesn't this little girl leave? Why is she staying where she is? Is it because she has a granny that is too weak to draw the water, too weak to kill the chicken, and too weak to cook it? But this little girl is blessed just because she still has a granny—that's more than most children have. Once the granny dies, there will be an empty house with a few chickens outside. Her community would like to have the house, and a little girl alone has no rights. What might happen to this child is horrendous to think about.

The Tribe of Bullies

The other tribe of children is a tribe of bullies, often made up of young boys and a few girls who have been abused by neighbors and family, and whose inheritances and homes have been stolen by other relatives. The boys are grudgingly fed a meal. These boys have lost everything: mom, dad, grandparents, and in many cases, some of their siblings. They've lost their homes, their inheritance, anything that is familiar, and any kindness in the earth. Perhaps these children have never been to school, but they might start going at the age of thirteen or fourteen. They're put in the first grade. Who can blame them when they are filled with anger? It is easy then for the bully nature to be exhibited—and it can come out in horrific ways.

A recent headline in a Swazi paper reported that a thirteen-year-old boy raped a five-year-old girl in the classroom while other children watched and several six-year-old boys held her down. The teacher had stepped out and gone to the office. Thank God, another boy from another class walked past the doorway and saw what was happening and told someone. If he had not, every little boy in that classroom might have raped this child. Then every boy would have tasted sex out of season, and every girl in the class would have seen that there is nothing they can do when such a scenario plays out. They would know that they could expect the same treatment.

These are the realities of uncared-for orphans who have not psychologically processed their loss and bereavement. Our task at New Hope Centre is to help the children unlock their grief before it consumes them and destroys everyone and everything in their path. Daily, we walk our children through the grieving process so they can get to the other side and become children who know their Heavenly Father and are confident of His love and provision for them.

What we invest in our children, we invest in our communities as well. Our greatest resource is the children of New Hope Centre. Regularly on Tuesdays, we go out to schools in the area. Our children create skits and teachings on the issues these orphans face, such as loss and grief. They share what they have learned about their Heavenly Father and how He has given each one keys to break through. They sing, dance, and spend time talking to the school children. We also talk about bullying and anger with them. We talk about depression and forgiveness. We encourage the children to be honest with their feelings. We try to give hope to those who feel cheated of life and a future. We let them know that while many of the reactions they are having are part of the grieving process, they don't have to be emotionally stuck in a sad and angry place.

Camps

We wish we could take in more children, but we simply do not have room or resources. While we may not be able to give every orphan a home, we try to do as much as we can to reach out to them and give them a temporary respite from their problems. One way we do this is through camps. We rent a huge tent from the police. We give opportunities for orphans who do not live at New Hope Centre to come and stay for a week. While they are with us, we teach them about nutrition, hygiene, how to purify water, and other necessary life skills that they can take home with them. Even more importantly, we give them an opportunity to heal through memory work.

A memory can hold a lot of trauma, and it can be the very thing keeping them from hope. So one of the first things we work through is identifying the "monster" in their lives. We then help them to confront the monsters that torment them and bring them pain. For Tirzah, the monster was imminent death stalking her, and it left her in despair.

We bring the children through dealing with what the monster is, and we teach them about the Superhero in their life who can defeat their nemesis. That Superhero's name is Jesus, and it is not His will that these children suffer or die. He has the wisdom and grace to bring them out of the pain of their memories so that they can have a hope and a future. The changes that can come to these children in only a few days are truly amazing. In our recent winter camp with forty-seven orphan children from the north, east, south, and central Swaziland, we administered the *25-Item Resilience Scale* test by Gail M. Wagnild and Heather M. Young (1993). The pre- and post-tests showed an increased score in the resilience of sixty percent of the children, and an increased level of resilience in thirty percent. This is tremendous success, and as we follow up on these children in the schools, we hope to measure their progress after another three months. In our recent meeting with the head teachers, they reported that every child who attended camp has changed. They exhibit more responsibility. Those who failed repeatedly in their grade have passed this year. One who was a notorious vandal has become the role model of integrity and justice, without having to repeat the year for the first time. We are rejoicing over these amazingly positive reports, especially since we had asked the head teachers to choose the most problematic children in the school for the camp.

There is something wonderful and significant about our orphans reaching out to other orphans. Our motto has been "Today's Orphans, Tomorrow's Leaders," but at our camps, when I see our youngsters exhibiting leadership, I know I have already glimpsed into tomorrow. No mother could be more proud than I am of these little ones as they make a difference community by community, school by school, throughout the country.

Lord of the Flies ended in tragedy, and Swaziland has tasted more tragedy than any nation ever should. With one of the highest HIV infections rates in the world, the sheer weight of the numbers would indicate that our story will end the same as the *Lord of the Flies*. But I don't believe this is God's will or destiny for these children. I believe He holds the key, He holds the hearts of those who can help, and He is able to turn this tale of despair and destruction into one of hope and redemption. I believe our children have a major part to play in the redemption of Swaziland. I believe if you are reading this book, you too have a part to play in turning a story into a miracle not seen or heard of among the family of nations.

Chapter 6

A New Name Written Down

There she stood at the gate—unkempt, dirty, and skinny to the point of emaciation. Even from a distance one could see the sores and scars on her skin. She was covered with scabies and had huge infected sores that she scratched as she stood waiting. In one hand she clutched a plastic bag filled with the sum total of her worldly goods. In the other hand she clutched a rolled-up piece of paper.

I was home alone at the time. Uncle Andile opened the gate to let her in and brought her up to the house. Straight away, we went to get her some food. While she was eating, I tried to find out more about her. Unlike most of the children who arrive at the home without documentation, she had that precious piece of paper with her. She handed it to me, and I quickly saw that it had been signed by her granny. It stated that in the event of her death, she wanted this child to go to New Hope Centre. I knew nothing about this child, but she knew all about New Hope Centre. She and her granny had attended the official opening of the New Hope Centre and Ministries in March, 2003. She even knew that each child who comes to the home receives a new name. She had already chosen hers.

"I want to be Anastasia," she said.

Anastasia

When we bring children into our family, we try to choose a biblical name that has a special meaning. Anastasia had chosen a name not found in the Bible, but the entire Bible is in the meaning of her name.

To see her made me want to weep. Not only did she have scabies, a skin infection caused by tiny parasites burrowing under the skin and then coming out to move to a new spot during the night, but she had scratched the sores with filthy fingernails. Now the sores were infected and oozing pus. Her body was covered with boils due to poor nutrition, lack of vitamins, and limited hygiene. So tiny, so alone, so vulnerable; what was this little girl's sad story?

After she had tried to eat, we went to the preschool room where I gave her some toys so she could play while we talked. We had already learned that one of the best ways to bring children out of their shell was to let them do what comes most naturally—play. Many of the children who come to us don't know how to play, and have to be taught. They catch on quickly. Knowing what to do with a bright, shiny toy, building blocks, and even holding a crayon are foreign concepts to them. Anastasia was one of those children who did not know how to play, and that told me a lot about her right away.

She didn't say much as I handed her the food and toys. She ate only a few mouthfuls of her sandwich, and then put it away. In a short time, she was hungry again; she ate a quarter of the sandwich and put it away. This process repeated itself every forty-five minutes or so. I realized that her stomach had shrunk, and it was likely she hadn't had a complete meal in years. She probably had survived by stealing one handful of food at a time.

I took her to see her room and showed her how to make her bed. She was in awe. I am sure she had never had a bed of any kind before, especially not one made up with clean sheets, a comforter, and a pillow. A friend of mine, Alison Brandt, who is a missionary teaching in Macau (Southern China), had just sent some brand new girls' clothes, and we found some garments that fit her. When she saw the clothing, she began to show some signs of life. She chose what she wanted and hung her new clothes in her wardrobe.

It is amazing to me that God not only rescues each child, but provides for them, sometimes even before they arrive here. It seems every clothing donation we receive comes just in time for each new arrival, even though we never know how old, big, or small our new arrival will be. It is such a joy to give a dirty, skinny child who has been discarded by society a beautiful new garment to wear. That new garment is a first step in restoring their dignity and worth, while it also gives them something to care for because it belongs to them. We had just received a package of clothes from a friend of mine in Australia. These clothes were clean and brand new, but most of all, they fit Anastasia, and she loved them.

I bathed her, and it was then I saw the extent of her sores. There were boils on her bottom and around her vagina. I knew too well how boils caused by a virus had gotten to those areas of her body. I knew too well that many of the children in our home have been raped and abused, and this eight-year-old child had already experienced more than most children. I washed her all over with an antiseptic wash called Savlon. I treated her infected wounds with ointments and covered the sores with Band-Aids®. By the time the other children arrived home, she had been washed, dressed in her new clothes, and was ready for them to begin engaging her in play. At first she was quite withdrawn, but soon she caught on and began to play with others.

A few days later, I took her to the clinic to get treatment for her sores and scabies. She also had worms. Of course, she had shared her parasites with the other children at the centre, so we engaged in all-out war against scabies, the little skin mites. Every night when the children showered, we had to cover their bodies from head to toe with medicated soap suds. They don't wash the lather off but rather let it dry. This creates a barrier the bugs must chew through. It poisons the bugs, and in a few days they are all gone. The boils, on the other hand, took months to heal. After a while, Anastasia was free from skin disease, but to this day she is still trying to gain weight.

It wasn't until her outward scars began to heal that she began to tell us her story. It happened like this. After the death of her parents, like most children left without parents, she was sent to live with her granny.

Grannies are often the last vital link to love and family that a child has. But many of these older grandmothers cannot bear such a heavy load, as they may inherit several children at the same time. At a time in their lives when they should be thinking of slowing down and being cared for by their children, Swaziland's *gogos* are required to nurse their ailing adult children and care for their orphaned grandchildren. The care of an AIDS patient is extremely difficult, and on top of that, the grandparents must often go to some distant spot to fetch water and firewood. They must cook, clean, and raise grandchildren—all without adequate funds. They quickly become a tapped-out resource as their family dies around them. Most of them have to find whatever work they can, no matter how demeaning it might be.

Knowing her granny's frail health, Anastasia begged that she be sent to live at New Hope Centre when her granny died. Her granny came and completed the applications for her to come to New Hope Centre upon her death. But when her granny died, these documents were ignored. She was sent to live at another homestead far from the place she and her granny had lived. There she became a servant girl and experienced much abuse.

Somehow, miraculously, she managed to escape and find her way back to her granny's house. When she got there, she found the piece of paper that would redeem her beaten-down life. Then she began the walk that would bring her to our gate. It was a long journey, one this little girl made on foot. Only God could have given her the strength and determination to do what she did. With only a plastic grocery bag of belongings, and a rolled up piece of paper in her hand, she walked miles to find us. Somehow she had found her way home—to us—before we knew her.

In her mind, Anastasia did not know the meaning of the name that she had chosen, but in her spirit she knew. Anastasia means "resurrection life." This scraggly-looking child, so worn and beaten down, knew deep in her soul that there was hope for a new life. There would be resurrection for her, and she wanted that more than anything else.

Today, Anastasia is a delightful, energetic child who loves to dance her praises to our God. She is studying ballet, and earned a silver award in the Royal School of Ballet exams last year. As her lithe body moves around the floor, one cannot help but think that she was born to dance, exalting her Maker.

Joseph

We never know when they will come or from where or how they will arrive. Some have been dropped off at our gate without any explanation. Some, like Anastasia, Noah, and Jesse, come to us because parents and grandparents know there is hope for their children within our gates. We only know that since we have opened our doors, we have become known around the country. Perhaps it's our name, "New Hope Centre," that promises hope in a country so devoid of hope that it causes us to stand out and gain attention. It makes no difference how they come. We are blessed when we can take them in. What a tragedy it would be if we had to turn anyone away.

Each child's arrival is different from those who have come before. Joseph was a special delivery child, and at one-and-a-half years, he was our smallest. He was found along the highway by a man driving a small truck. Joseph was beside his mother on the side of the road. She was having convulsions. The man loaded both of them into his truck and drove them to our home where he dumped them just inside the gate. The child was full of sores, and he was in a state of shock as he and his mum lay on the ground where they had been dumped by the "Good Samaritan" in the truck. We didn't know where they had come from or who they were, so we took them to the police station to register them as unknown persons, and then on to the hospital. The woman was suffering from severe meningitis, dehydration, shingles, and AIDS. She was admitted to the hospital, and we took Joseph home with us.

Normally, we don't take children under the age of two, as we don't have the staff or resources to care for them. But Joseph stole every heart in the home, including the children's, so we made an exception to our rule, and Joseph became part of our family.

Emmanuel, a young Swazi man, loved Joseph. Emmanuel was a youth volunteer in his community when he came to work with us. While he worked with us, he studied early childhood education part-time at the Swedish Free Evangelical Training Centre. It is totally unusual for a man to study such a subject. But just as God had gathered our children, he also gathered our staff. It was a big sacrifice to work in a children's home, but God had called Emmanuel to be a big brother to our little ones. It was an important role, as many of these children have not known a brother's or a father's love. And no matter how much I loved the children, I could not be a big brother or a father to them. They needed Emmanuel in their lives.

Emmanuel came to me that first night and asked if he could name our new arrival Joseph. Since Joseph was so young, and non-verbal at the time, it was not feasible to consult with him in the choice of his name. Much like his biblical namesake, he had been abandoned and left for dead—but God had another plan, one of redemption. Even though our little one had a rather bumpy start to life, we were sure that, like Joseph of the Bible, he would fulfill a special calling.

Emmanuel took the child and washed him as we went to search for blankets and clothes. When we tried to feed him solid food, we soon realized that he couldn't yet eat. So we put together a semi-liquid mixture that he heartily slurped from a cup.

Joseph made no sounds—nothing—no babbling, no words, he didn't even cry. It was pretty obvious he was still in shock. He just sat and stared at us with big eyes. He couldn't sleep either. Perhaps he was too tense or perhaps he was waiting for his mother. He would doze off for a few minutes, and then wake again and go on staring. When at last exhaustion hit him and he surrendered to sleep, he was on his knees under a blanket. We weren't sure what we should do. Finally, we sat with him all night, night after night, praying or singing in tongues over him.

The next day after his arrival, we washed the little guy from head to toe again and dressed him in new clothes. We had to carry him everywhere, because even though he could walk, he would just stand and stare. We put him in the preschool with the other children. Miss Tracie and Miss Zanele and the children would hug him and try to bring him out of his shell. But still he would only sit and stare.

This went on for five days. Then on the fifth day we heard him speak—just words. As the weeks progressed he became more confident and began to play. At times he would smile and laugh. At other times he would sit and weep, especially at night when he was tormented with nightmares in which he would say his mother was calling him. One night we found him sitting at the gate in a fit of terror. He was crying, and when we finally calmed him down, he told us his mother was calling for him. While he clearly didn't want to leave, still he was drawn to the gate by the voice of his mother. Big brother Emmanuel found him and held him for a while, then brought him back to bed and explained to the child that he didn't have to leave. This happened again and again over a period of two to four months. Sometimes he would come running to us, saying, "They are coming to get me." He would be inconsolable at first, but after taking him in our arms, praying over him in the Spirit, and assuring him that no one would or could take him from us, he would begin to relax and sleep through the night.

Nights are the most exhausting times for us. We usually have two problems to deal with: bed-wetting and nightmares. Both come from the same source: insecurity and fear. Just understanding that helps us to respond to each child with mercy, compassion, and affirmation of who they are and how they are loved. It's something we have to reinforce over and over. We wake each child to use the toilet at around 11 P.M. to alleviate the bed-wetting and the shame each child has when this happens. Alleviating nightmares is another matter. Nightmares are common in children, but our children have nightmares of another kind. They are the kind of nightmares where real issues and the trauma of their pasts come to the surface. These can be terrifying for the child, but helpful for us as we piece together their issues and help them heal.

Most dreams come from two sources: inner consciousness (God speaking something to bring truth), or nightmares that come from the pit of hell. The latter was Joseph's case. Like many children in Swaziland, he had been dedicated to false gods and demons. Often, a parent or grandparent will make a covenant with demonic forces. The baby is held over a fire and dedicated (some may remember this in the TV series *"Roots"*). This is a common ritual in Swaziland, but it creates all matter of chaos when they come into our home. We have to deal with that whole spiritual realm when a child comes into our care. It takes time. So when a child wakes up screaming and crying, the big sister, big brother, or houseparent who is in the room must immediately go to them and talk them through it. This is only accomplished through much prayer. In many cases, though, these nightmares help us unlock the trauma buried deep in their memory. This takes discernment, but as we listen to their stories and encourage them to talk about their dreams, we often have a revelation of what lies at the source of their trauma. We pray with each child for the interpretation of the dream, because we don't want to lose any truth that is in these dreams—truth that could set a child free.

Today, Joseph stands tall and confident. He smiles and laughs, knowing that he is safe and secure in the Abraham family and is destined for greatness.

Ruth Means "Friend"

Nightmares were the case with Ruth, our second-youngest at the time. When she came to us, she would scream night and day, day and night. I've learned in the years of dealing with children that there are different kinds of screams. There are screams for attention: "I want my own way and will to be done." There are screams that are defense mechanisms, and they come when the child is caught doing something he or she shouldn't be doing. And then there are the screams that come out of history—out of the memories lodged deep in the soul.

Before we deal with any child, we must pray for discernment. We need to know what kind of scream is coming from the child. How we respond to that scream is crucial. We don't want to reinforce bad behavior, but if it is a scream out of pain and terror, then we want to make sure that the child gets proper attention. The best way to find out what kind of scream is being uttered is to take a child on your lap and enfold the child with strong sure love. That means we sit with them, our arms enfolded around them, while they scream and scream until the power of that emotion comes out. This takes a lot of patience, prayer, and mercy, because in some cases, it takes three or four weeks of howling, crying, and sobbing before this coming out occurs.

It is crucial to see this process through. If we short-circuit the process by asking the screaming child what is wrong, and if they cannot tell us, we simply tell them to quit crying. We can't afford to do that, because at the root, these children are crying as though it is the end of the world, and given what Ruth had lived through, it very nearly was the end of the world for her.

Both of Ruth's parents died and she was being cared for by a child-minder until her grandfather died. Then there was no one to pay the child-minder. She suffered sexual and emotional abuse where she was staying. At last, a pastor referred her to New Hope Centre. Every time we woke her, whether in the morning or at naptime, she screamed. If we corrected her bad behavior, she screamed. And sometimes she screamed for what seemed to us to be no reason at all. She would just scream and scream for an hour, or two or three.

It was disturbing, but after weeks of screaming, we finally learned what the issue was. She was afraid of being conscious—being awake and alive—because everything in life was so overwhelming to her. She had not yet dealt with the grief of her young life, and this was how that grief manifested itself.

Miss Tracie and Miss Zanele were very patient and gentle with her. They would hold her and sit with her and talk things through with her day after day. As they held her, they prayed in tongues and communicated their strength to her through strong, sure hugs. We don't give wishy-washy hugs at New Hope

Centre, because these children need strength—the strength only a strong hug will give them. When they are being held in a firm, secure, and unshakable embrace, they are able to rest. It is as if they are being taken back to the time when they were infants wrapped tightly and snuggly in a blanket. There in our arms, they can feel our heartbeat, and it communicates to them that they will be all right. They will make it. Muscle to muscle, bone to bone, they absorb our strength into their own souls. The need for security is one of the most basic needs of mankind. And at New Hope Centre, it isn't just the young ones who need hugs. It is all of the children, young and old.

So, scream by scream, hug by hug, we come to know their tragic stories, and we begin bit by bit to unwind the cords that bind these children. Today, Ruth is quite a different little girl than the one that first came to New Hope Centre. Her screams are gone, the pouting is gone, and she has grown to be a lovely, helpful, clever young leader of her preschool classmates, reliable and trustworthy.

A little child, a new name, a new home, and the awesome power of God's Holy Spirit are redeeming the "years the locust have eaten." The awful years of abuse, fear, and unbelievable emotional pain drop away as our children are redeemed by God's love and power.

> *I will repay you for the years the locusts have eaten—*
> *the great locust and the young locust,*
> *the other locusts and the locust swarm—*

My great army that I sent among you.
You will have plenty to eat, until you are full,
and you will praise the name of the LORD your God,
who has worked wonders for you;
never again will my people be shamed.

—Joel 2:25–26

PART III
LIVING IN FAMILY

Chapter 7

GOD THE FATHER

His father was a policeman stationed far from the home-stead, and his mother died, leaving young Caleb aching and desperate for someone to love and care for him. He longed for a father. Like most of the other children in our home, when he became an orphan, he was passed from family member to family member, and then finally to strangers who made him a "slave" to herd their cattle. At times, he would run away for days. He was confused, and lacked the security that only a father's love can provide. Finally he ran away for good, and lived as a street kid in Swaziland's capital city of Mbabane. But it was too much for him, and he decided to return to try to find his father.

He walked for days to the place he thought his father might be, only to discover that his father had died not long before. His aunt was there, but she, being unemployed and having eight children of her own, turned him away to go and fend for himself. The police referred Caleb to New Hope Centre. And what a gift he is! Caleb is warm, intelligent, kind to the other children, and friendly to all he meets. He's a swimmer, a talented singer and dancer, and looks forward to the day when he can fulfill his calling to be a pastor. He is already busy preaching and teaching the Word in our home and in the community. He was Camp Director for the Hope Camp this past winter, and preached in the evenings. Recently, he and Debrah were invited as keynote speakers at the Lobamba Christian Family Church's annual youth camp.

In our home there are big brothers, big sisters, uncles, aunties, and housemothers. But there is only one Father. God expresses His heart for orphans by calling Himself a Father to the fatherless. In Psalm 68:4–5, the writer tells us:

> *Sing to God, sing praise to his name,*
> *extol him who rides on the clouds*
> *his name is the LORD—*
> *and rejoice before him.*
> *A father to the fatherless, a defender of widows,*
> *is God in his holy dwelling.*

So while God is Father to us all, He singles out orphans for a special acknowledgement. He knows their sorrow. He knows what it means to them not to have an earthly father to protect and love them. He knows that without a father, a child loses his or her security and identity and is vulnerable to the wickedness of this world. It is for this reason that He gives us clear directives about how to care for the orphans and widows. There can be no excuses. He says:

> *Religion that God our Father accepts as pure and faultless is this: to look after orphans and widows in their distress and to keep oneself from being polluted by the world.*
> —James 1:27

Or, in the beautiful language of the King James Version:

Pure religion and undefiled before God and the Father is this, to visit the fatherless and widows in their affliction, and to keep himself unspotted from the world.

"Pure religion and undefiled" seems not to be about more prayer or a better quality of prayer. It is not about more or improved Bible reading. It is about visiting the fatherless and widows, no matter what their affliction—even AIDS. It is looking after those widows and children who are in distress. As we seek to obey this command, we still need to understand the plight of orphans, especially orphans in Swaziland, where by the year 2010 it is estimated that there will be 200,000 orphans out of a shrinking population of 860,000 people.

The Swazi government has made various attempts to give some help, but it has no solutions to this flood of disenfranchised children other than to conduct studies to identify where the largest concentrations of these children are located, and to identify volunteers and authorities who can be counted on to implement ideas and programs to meet this growing deluge of need.

One of the areas with the greatest problem is Manzini, near the place New Hope Centre is located. Manzini is the largest city in Swaziland. Street children are flocking there along with migrant workers, hoping to find work. Orphan children are pressed into slave labor as the labor pool of available adults shrinks due to AIDS deaths. The plight of the street children is unfathomable to most of us. They are hungry, filled with disease, and every moment of their lives is threatened by violence and abuse. These children are called "Orphans and Vulnerable Children" (OVC).

In terms of physically staying alive, the first and most immediate need of these children is food. Various organizations have opened "care points" where orphan children can come once a day for a meal, but many do not come, because of the stigma associated with being exposed as an orphan. At New Hope Centre, we have started what we hope will be copied throughout Swaziland. We cultivate a small garden to grow fresh vegetables, which provide nourishment and vitamins. Initially, we help with a sack of dirt, a two-liter coke bottle of water, and a few seedlings. Even a five-year-old can care for this kind of vegetable garden. Success in a small way gives the confidence to try a "real" garden in the ground. With help from volunteers from Heart for Africa, we helped six homesteads make a five-meter-by-five-meter vegetable garden, with a fence to keep the cattle and goats out. Since then, other groups have come and helped, so we now have eighty five-by-five vegetable gardens in homes around New Hope Centre. We have learned methods used in the ancient times of the Essenes in Israel: conserving water, enriching the soil, and reaping massive cabbages, carrots, and spinach from a small patch, using "God's blanket." We cover it with cut grass to keep the moisture in the soil. We have planted fruit trees that have yet to bear fruit (except for a big mango tree that has been here for a long time), but at least they are in the ground and growing. We also have chickens to provide eggs and meat, and we have added four milk cows and two calves. Not only do we hope to feed our own brood of youngsters, but we hope for excess to sell at the markets. We are now helping orphans in twenty schools in the eastern part of Swaziland to do the same. We hope, as teams and friends visit, to begin with six gardens at orphan homes at each school.

When we started at New Hope Centre, God sent what we needed through the mail, through people sending a few clothes and shoes at a time. We did not have funds for school shoes or school uniforms, but each and every child had a few clothes ready for them upon arrival. Clothes shelter us from the burning sun of summer, and also protect from the cold winds and nights of winter. We can never have "enough" clothes, so to speak. Our own children often empty their wardrobes so we can

Dr. Elizabeth Hynd, a "Deborah" in Swaziland.

Joyfully watering our vegetable garden.

Rev. Dr. June McKinney with two leaders of tomorrow.

First Christian church built in Swaziland at Mahamba.

The children's home—a prophetic Noah's Ark.

Dr. Samuel Hynd examining one of the family.

Happy Overcomers playfully running.

The African elephant, keeper of the kingdom.

give to children in the community who have nothing. When we bring orphans to camp, many are too ashamed to come, as they have no clothes, so it is an important part of caring to be able to give each camper a couple days' supply of clothes: a sweater or a jacket, a pair of shoes and socks. If only we could collect containers full of clothes from garage sales in the USA and other countries, we could make a huge difference in the lives and self-image of thousands and thousands of children.

An overwhelming need is for children to get an education. Education is not free in Swaziland. Fees must be paid, or you are sent home. The children also need funds for uniforms and school supplies. Without these things, the children are taunted for the way they look, and because they don't have basic supplies. They are often shunned if their parents have died of AIDS. It is discouraging enough for orphans to get *to* school. The bullying and discrimination they receive *at* school makes it almost impossible to get the education so important to their future and survival. Many give up, and live out their lives uneducated. We will talk more in a later chapter about how we are meeting our orphans' need for education and training in leadership.

Orphan children in Swaziland are also tremendously lacking in health care. Health centers are too widely scattered, and transportation to them is costly and time-consuming. These children are at risk for so many diseases in addition to AIDS. There is cholera from drinking contaminated water. There is malaria from infected mosquitoes in some areas of the country. Bilharzia (parasitic chronic disease) is a common problem, as children wash in the rivers and streams. There are childhood illnesses for which they have not been vaccinated. And in many cases, even if they have been vaccinated, their immunity card has been lost and the health ministry does not issue a new one. Without that card, no one knows if the child has been immunized or not.

But even more than all these losses, we need to understand what losing a father means to these children. It is different from losing a mother. Most assume that the two are interchangeable. They are not. When a child loses his father, he loses his identity. It was the father's seed that gave him life, and it was his name that gave the child identity. When we do seminars, we will often brainstorm and ask orphans what it means to lose a mother, and then we brainstorm what it means to lose a father. This is when everyone comes undone. They just lose it.

Why? Because whether he was a good father or a bad father or even an indifferent one, just to know he or she has a father gives great security to the child. The role of the father is to be a refuge and a defense in times of trouble. And while many fathers fail in this area, it helps the child know there is someone to run to. So in losing their father, they lose their defender. They lose their identity and security. Women have no rights in traditional Swazi culture, so if you have lost a father, even though your mother may still be alive, you have no rights to property or any other possessions. As long as there is a father present, you know that your home is yours, your property is yours, and your possessions are safe. But when you lose a father, you truly have lost everything.

That's why God's promise to be a *father to the fatherless* is so vital to these children. How do we communicate that to a child who has lost so much? How do we communicate it to a child who has been beaten and violated? How do we communicate it to a Caleb?

It's not easy, but when you get close to God's heart for the orphan, you begin to understand the amazing capacity of love and grace with which He wants to fill your own imperfect heart. Indeed, you have to first know and believe that God is your Father, before you can ever hope to impart that truth to orphans. It is out of the fullness of your own love for the orphan that love and grace can be imparted to him or her.

To some extent, we are all orphans if we have never come to understand the fatherhood that God has provided for us through the sacrifice of His Son Jesus. As such spiritual orphans, we too have no entitlements to the gifts and promises of God. We too are bereft of identity, and of the safety God the Father offers us. The good news is that God is seeking us out. Through His Holy Spirit, He is drawing us to Himself. A. W. Tozer, a great theologian of the twentieth century, said:

> We pursue God because, and only because, He has first put an urge within us that spurs us to the pursuit. "No man can come to me," said our Lord Jesus, "except the Father which hath sent me draw him . . ." The impulse to pursue God originates with God, but the outworking of that impulse is our following hard after Him. All the time we are pursuing Him we are already in His hand: "Thy right hand upholdeth me."[1]

So it is with our children. While they pursue an earthly father, God, the Heavenly Father, is pursuing them for His own purposes. Though God is invisible, children have a great capacity for imagination. A child can move from the physical world to the invisible spiritual realm effortlessly. They will "get it" once they know about the invisible Father in heaven. We spend a lot of time with each child, identifying and working through who God the Father is, how He cares for them, and His desire to provide for them. There are so many promises of His father's heart and examples of His love and grace in the Bible. He promises to hide them under a cover, to defend them, and to rescue them from death. He declares that He is their shelter and that He will hide them under His wing where the sun can't burn them and the arrows can't hit them, because they

---

[1] A. W. Tozer, *The Pursuit of God*, Christian Publications, Camp Hill, Pennsylvania, ©1993, p. 11.

have put their trust in Him. God is the Father who sees us as the apple of His eye, precious, sensitive, unique, and special; He is the Father who rejoices over us with singing (Zeph. 3:17). But these will just be words to them unless we who teach them to know these truths in the reality of our own lives. Both our spirits and their spirits must be activated and animated by the precious Holy Spirit. Only then can the child receive and know that these truths of God the Father are real and to be trusted.

The children must learn and know that the spirit realm is more real than the physical one. C. S. Lewis described it so beautifully in *The Last Battle* in the Chronicles of Narnia series when he said that what we suppose is real—such as our life here on earth—is only a shadow of the reality that is eternal. A child can understand that concept quite easily. Adults have a more difficult time. And that's why the Word says, *A little child shall lead them,* or, *The kingdom of heaven belongs to such as these.* Children often grasp what an adult only grapples toward. Many older people have lost touch with imagination and the realities of the spirit realm, and it's difficult for them to activate those things from the time when they were children.

Father to the Fatherless

When Caleb came to us, what he lacked most was an identity. This is the case with most of our orphans. When they lose their earthly fathers, they lose their identity. We are determined and committed to help the children regain a sense of who they are and what God intended for them in this life.

A study by the psychologist Abraham Maslow in 1943 determined the needs of individuals to become whole, self-accepting people—people who have an identity and who can then go on to solve problems and be creative. He formed his study of basic human needs into a pyramid that looked something like this:

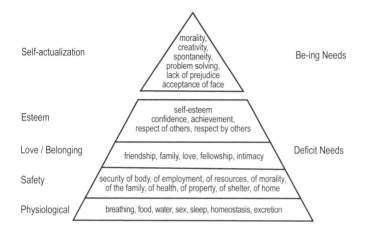

(Source: Wikipedia)

The four lower levels (physiological, safety, love/belonging, and esteem) are grouped together as being associated with deficit needs. Deficit needs, such as food, shelter, family, and self-esteem, must first be met before the upper level of be-ing needs comes into focus. When a child is safe and knows he is accepted and his identity is intact, then he can work on personal growth. And once the child moves up the pyramid, the needs at the lower levels will no longer be the priority they once were. More of his energy can be directed toward creativity, spontaneity, and problem-solving—the be-ing needs. It was Maslow's theory that every person has an internal "push" towards wholeness. In the case of the D-needs (physiological, safety, love/belonging, and self-esteem), a person is motivated to push towards obtaining each of these because of the lack in their lives. Hunger or lack of food would push an individual to plough the field, milk the cow, feed the chickens, or steal from their neighbors. By some means, a human being would push to meet the most basic (the physiological) need, as without this level they would cease to live. Similarly, the absence of safety and security would push the person to make skins for clothing, or build a corrugated iron shed to keep them warm or shelter them from the rain. These may be the case, but in the plight of overwhelming despair, many orphaned and abandoned children give up before they ever reach self-esteem or respect. The be-ing needs that Maslow believed in only concerned a person once the four deficit needs were met. The force pushing the be-ing needs is not from a deficit force but from the need of your very existence to BE a healthy, happy, creative, satisfied, and content person.

In our ministry with our children and community children, or those in schools where we minister, the deficit needs and be-ing needs must be actively and diligently worked on. However, as a human being, the be-ing needs are the most essential, because we are made in the image of our Creator.

We might take issue with the word "*self*-esteem," for in a culture where identity—who you are—is based on who your father is and whether you have a father or not, finding esteem through your self is problematic. That is why understanding the fatherhood of God is vitally important to our orphans. They are not orphans in His sight. They are children of the Most High Ruler of the universe. He gives them value. He gives them esteem and identity. And so, too, if any of us try to gain our identity through what we can do or our intelligence or our beauty, we will come up sadly lacking, for no one can give us worth or value except our Father in heaven.

In the case of our children, we need to communicate to them who created them, what He's like, and the value they have to Him. They may have heard the story of creation, but missed the greater truth that they were made in the image of God.

So God created man in his own image, in the image of God he created him; male and female he created them.
—Genesis 1:27

And not only were they made, but they were thought of long before the beginning of time. Before their mother and father got together, before they were formed in the womb, God was thinking about them and fine-tuning their destinies just as He did the prophet Jeremiah.

Before I formed you in the womb I knew you,
before you were born I set you apart;
I appointed you as a prophet to the nations.
—Jeremiah 1:5

As our children go out into the community, this is the strongest message they carry to other fatherless children. More than the goods or food supplies they deliver, this message— that God is the orphan's Father—brings life. Our Abraham family living on Bethany Mountain at New Hope Centre has a mighty Father who saved them from sure destruction and brought them to safety, security, and love.

Don't misunderstand. God is not a substitute father—a backup when we don't have an earthly one. Indeed, our earthly fathers are supposed to teach us about God the Father. They are to model emotionally, physically, and relationally what it means to have a God with whom we can relate. *Our Father who art in heaven, hallowed be thy name, thy kingdom come, thy will be done on earth as it is in heaven. Give us today our daily bread and forgive us for our trespasses as we forgive those who trespass against us. Lead us not into temptation but deliver us from evil. For thine is the kingdom the power and the glory, forever and ever, Amen.* But many fathers fail. And there are those of us who don't know who our earthly fathers are, or they are absentee fathers, so we don't even have a father to disappoint us in the first place. Many of us walk through life with our heads hanging down, depressed because our earthly fathers have fallen short. Some of us become bitter and angry, and some even become self-destructive.

You can see, then, why at New Hope Centre we spend so much time on the idea of God the Father being the children's father. He is the One who thought about them before the beginning of time, and created who they were inside the thoughts of His Spirit. When they can accept that truth, from that point on they can start to see the fuller picture. They can draw into the identity of not just the physical, but the thought process behind their creation. They begin to ask: "What was God thinking of when He created me?" "What did He invest in me?" "How did He gift me?"

And the wonderful thing is that God, by His Holy Spirit, will activate these things as we talk about them and ponder or meditate on them. Our children discover very early on that their personhood is not based on the negative, harsh words spoken over them in the past. Words such as: "You'll never succeed," "You're talking too much," "You're a burden," have diminished their sense of worth. These words are often spoken over children in impoverished countries, where they are seen as one more mouth to feed, one more body to clothe, one more costly child to educate, and that is about all. We tell them, "You know what? Your Father owns the cattle on a thousand hills." That has real meaning in Swaziland, where cattle are valuable commodities used in bartering and marital dealings. Having cattle denotes wealth. We tell our children, "Your Father creates the gold. The silver and gold are His. If you need silver and gold, He can create them for you. The fact that there is gold under the earth doesn't mean it's not available to you. So if gold and silver are what we need, we can speak them into existence through the power of the Holy Spirit."

God the Provider

Soon, our children come to know God as the provider of every need, not just theoretically, but in practice. It's how each of us at New Hope Centre lives—by faith that He will meet every need. Everything we have comes through prayer and trusting God. If we have a need, like paying the electric bill, many times the bill gets paid on time, but at other times it does not. If we have no money to pay it, we speak with the children and everyone agrees to pray until the need is met.

Our children's prayers are powerful. One volunteer from Canada went home. She wanted to come back, but was unsure that she would have enough money to make the trip. The children prayed that when she got home, God would provide the money for her ticket the first week, and that she would know what He wanted her to do. Sure enough, when she got home, she checked her bank account, and there was enough money to buy her ticket. Miss Lindsay returned for another year.

Our children learn in such a firm and real way the amazing power of God's Holy Spirit to act in answer to their prayers, that they have no trouble communicating their faith to others. They communicate their faith to our volunteers and to other orphans in our community. They know that a biological dad may be dead, but Dad in heaven is an even greater defender and provider for them. Little by little and day by day, our children are getting to know the loving tenderness of their Heavenly Father. Caleb has learned to trust God as a faithful Father, and he is growing in wisdom and in favor with God and man.

Chapter 8

ABRAHAM'S FAMILY

One of the great promises of God is that He will set the solitary (the lonely) in families:

God sets the lonely in families,
he leads forth the prisoners with singing . . .
—Psalm 68:6

When God promised to be a Father to the fatherless, He didn't stop there. He knows our needs, He created us, and He knows the need each one of us has for a family. This is where the community and the church come in.

Our home is unique. We are a family. We all have the same family name. We are the "Abrahams." When we have a second home, the name will be the "Solomons." But that's a story yet to be written. In our home, everyone is a brother or sister. But when we minister to the children outside New Hope Centre, some are from child-headed families. That means the head of household may be ten or eleven years old. When these children come to our camp, we work with them, first of all, to understand how to communicate with God as father, provider, security, identity, defender, and creator.

We must also teach them about family—how God provides surrogate homes and families for us when we don't have one of our own. This is where we try to network with local churches. The church is the larger family to which we all belong, the Body of Christ. The church has succeeded in preaching the gospel of salvation, but hasn't always followed through on what Jesus preached. He said:

> I was a stranger and you did not invite me into your home. I was naked, and you didn't give me clothing. I was sick and in prison, and you did not visit me.
> —Matthew 25:43

There are households where children are still in their original homes that belonged to their dads, and where their communities have done what is right and let the children stay in their own homes, but those households often fall through the cracks. These are difficult, heartbreaking situations. Child-headed homes need the Kingdom of God to become real to them, too. They need the church. We are working through local schools in impoverished areas of the country to network orphans, schools, communities, and churches by mobilizing a team composed of two teachers, two caregivers, and two youth leaders. We are trying to work through this small team with local churches to include these children in their church family. The church can't fulfill the role of father, but it can fulfill the role of family and provide a pool of people who will watch over the orphaned children, making sure they have the care they need. There need to be people who make sure the children go to school, or if they are sick, take them to a medical centre. The church needs to make sure the basic needs of the orphans are met—needs such as food and clothing, and fees and uniforms for school. We are committed to seek out and find those in need, then work through the youth leaders in the schools, providing a catalyst for the church to take its role.

When God showed us that we were to find the destitute of the destitute, the Psalm 68 scripture became real. We are to look for the children who really are solitary. We are to seek out children who have lost their families and homes. We are to give shelter to those who have lost their place in life and don't know where they belong. Our home is the answer to God's Word to "set the solitary in families."

We wish we could rescue all the lonely orphans in Swaziland. We know there are thousands of children out there that we haven't found, and for whom we have no room or resources. The church must get involved to help. And it is not just the African church that must respond. While the church in the west has done much to answer the great need here, there is often a feeling of overwhelming helplessness that leads to inaction. There is a rationale that says, "We can't solve the problem. It's too big." And so we do nothing at all.

God has begun to touch hearts in America, Europe, and Australia, bringing partners alongside New Hope Centre. Volunteers have come to help by repairing a roof or a wall, planting a garden, testing vision for the children and the community, and bringing hope to the children just because they come. Some have come more than once, like Heart for Africa, GO-TEAMS, Africa Trust, Pellham Community Church, and Southbrook Community Church, to name some, while others have come once or come as individuals to give their time, love, talents, and resources. No one can measure what such simple acts of kindness mean to these children. It is evidence that God is watching over them. He has sent His people from the ends of the earth to bring them something as simple as a pot or a blanket, a prayer, or the wonder of encouragement and a smile.

Abundance

Our children don't have all the material things they crave. Some of their clothes are a bit threadbare. Shoes often go missing. But they are living in abundance—spiritual abundance. In other words, they are in a place where they can dance and be free and know that as they get in touch with God their Father, they are getting in touch with who they are. They have been created and adopted by God—cared for by Him. They can receive all that He has for them. Abundance is having enough for ourselves and enough to give away, and our children have that. They do not need to hoard the blessings of God. They can freely share the love of God with others. And they do.

We model abundant living in our family. Say a farmer brings us a truckload of oranges; there is no way we can consume them all. So we bundle them up in bags and give them to families around Bethany Mountain. Out of our abundance, we are able to give and bless others. As our children share with others, they learn to give of what they have. Jesus instructed that if you have two tunics, give one away. He didn't say to give both away. He just said to give the second shirt away. Our children do this literally. When we get clothing donations, it's the children who sort through them, and after the needs of the home are met, we give the rest of it away to the community. We give both practical and spiritual gifts to our neighbors out of the abundance God has given the children. When our children go into the community and speak about what God has done for them, they see the freedom, the abundance that has brought them out of the bondage of their tragic circumstances.

We would like to extend this sharing of abundance to communities other than our own, but to do so we would need more vehicles and more adults. Our children still need protection. We can't send them out alone to a world where people are angry, frustrated, and in despair. They would be vulnerable to harm. One of our children, Elijah, was rescued from such a situation, where a neighbor, for no good reason other than his own frustration, regularly beat the boy with a lead pipe. This person, bound in his own anger, took out his rage on this young child. We cannot let that happen by letting our children go out unattended. So, at this time, we are keeping this dream as a goal—to have enough transportation and adults to send out teams of children to communities other than our own, where they can share both the physical and spiritual abundance God has given them. Then they would have the honor and privilege of fulfilling what King Somhlolo said: "Eat the word and live."

All About Families

Most of us have grown up in families, and along the way, our parents may have failed. None of us gets to choose where or to whom we're born. If we had a choice, some of us would have chosen different families. Our parents failed us, their parents failed them, and so on back to the time of Adam and Eve, who began this cycle of failure.

God's original design for the family was that it be a nurturing nest, a place where you could test your strengths and work on your weaknesses until you were able to walk in the dignity, talents, and abilities God has invested in you. We have multiple generations of human beings who have grown up with a flawed design—a family that didn't work. Our attempts to create a family with children who have been highly damaged and left destitute and abused, increases our challenge. Add to that the fact that we who live and work with the children carry our own family breakdowns and failures. We all have a lot to learn. Noah is one child who for the first couple years he lived with us walked with stooped shoulders until God, through friends in Africa Equip, sponsored him to go to Birmingham, England. He and Caleb went for swim training, starting the preparation for the Olympics in 2012. During that month, he was special. He ate well, slept well, trained in the pool for two hours a day, and daily spent two hours with me working on the scriptures, learning that we are joint heirs with Jesus, born into His Spirit, seated in heavenly places with Him, born to be royal priests, kingly prophets, a holy nation, and a peculiar people belonging to God. He has returned now to Swaziland, and walks as if he were a king. There are no stooped shoulders, no apology for being who he is. He is a brother to Jesus, the King of Kings.

So we must all come together to learn what the father's role should be and what the role of the mother is. We read that we are to love God with all our heart and love our neighbor as ourselves. What does it mean to love? The words of the scripture are brief and simple, but the concept is complicated. It doesn't happen easily. If our mothers and fathers had learned how to love God like that, we would have a better clue as to how to "love God with all our heart and our neighbor as ourselves."

Paul gives us a clue as to what loving God and others is all about in 1 Corinthians 13. Here, he lists the main attributes of love:

> *If I speak in the tongues of men and of angels, but have not love, I am only a resounding gong or a clanging cymbal. If I have the gift of prophecy and can fathom all mysteries and all knowledge, and if I have a faith that can move mountains, but have not love, I am nothing. If I give all I possess to the poor and surrender my body to the flames, but have not love, I gain nothing.*
>
> *Love is patient, love is kind. It does not envy, it does not boast, it is not proud. It is not rude, it is not self-seeking, it is not easily angered, it keeps no record of wrongs. Love does not delight in evil but rejoices with the truth. It always protects, always trusts, always hopes, always perseveres.*

Love never fails. But where there are prophecies, they will cease; where there are tongues, they will be stilled; where there is knowledge, it will pass away. For we know in part and we prophesy in part, but when perfection comes, the imperfect disappears. When I was a child, I talked like a child, I thought like a child, I reasoned like a child. When I became a man, I put childish ways behind me. Now we see but a poor reflection as in a mirror; then we shall see face to face. Now I know in part; then I shall know fully, even as I am fully known.

And now these three remain: faith, hope and love. But the greatest of these is love.

In order to have a team of people who can take on the great mission of creating a home for orphans, we all need to have a commitment to press in to receive the kind of love the Apostle Paul talks about in the Corinthians passage. We must first receive this love into the core of our own being to be able to give it away to others.

Our home is not only a picture of how God puts the orphan into a family, it is also a picture of how He puts our team members into a family, and indeed how He put all of us into the family of those who believe. Our team—our family, if you like—is made up of nationals and internationals. Our dream is to have as many internationals as possible, so that our children can grow up understanding that the family of God is composed of Chinese, Indians, Kenyans, Greeks, Israelis, Americans, Canadians, Brazilians, and on and on. Presently as I write, we have a Korean, a Chinese, an Australian, two Brits, and two Canadians working with us. We would love to have volunteers come from every nation so that our children can understand that God is no respecter of persons. You may be of another race or language from anywhere in the world, and He will equip you with the same love, life, joy, peace, and hope. Combining internationals with Swazis is a tremendous mix, because grace *has* to abound. There are cultural and behavioral differences, language differences, and attitudinal differences, to name a few. And there are inevitable family conflicts. But if we are all children of God, we need to spend time learning what it means to live as a member of God's family—a citizen of His kingdom. As we learn the attributes of a citizen of heaven, we become what God intended us to be. God intended that what He established in heaven would also be established on earth. Jesus taught us to pray, "Thy kingdom come, thy will be done on earth as it is in heaven." So joy, peace, light, and love are what God desires us to have here on earth.

As we here at New Hope Centre work together as a team crossing cultural racial and gender barriers, it takes grace and an extending of mercy, love, and forgiveness. The training process requires that we honor the Word of God, learning to feel our spirit within us, being led by the Holy Spirit. Many of us bear an infantile spirit because we have insufficiently fed our spirits with the Word of God. We have yet to enter into true worship that leads into His presence and the courts of heaven. We have been reticent to build up ourselves by praying in tongues. Our spirits are juvenile.

God desires our spirits to be mighty so they can take dominion over our bodies and souls. They then become easily led by His Spirit. The process of becoming a team member is often a process of learning humility. Mother Teresa, the great defender of orphans, had her volunteers clean toilets for three weeks before entering into ministry with the precious ones on the street. This was her way of seeking out those graced with humility, qualified to join her family in ministry. While we don't require our volunteers to clean toilets, each one must learn that this whole experience is not about them. It is about the children, and the service they can provide to our children. This calls for an exercise of "dying" to self in many ways, firstly, by doing things for others you may never have done before, and by going without the comforts or crutches we use to cover old needs or problems in life. Living in a family exposes strengths and weaknesses in us, forcing us to walk in humility and in honor, preferring one another. There is plenty of room for volunteers to join this family and come under the banner of love. This is not a mushy kind of love, but a love that is strong, sure, honest, kind, and considerate. It is not a boastful love. While some may only come for a short term, there is always a place for them, much like it is in the family of God.

There's a saying that goes something like this: "God loves you, but I'm His favorite." We may smile at that statement, but I believe it is the truth when it comes to His heart for the orphan. That's why He is their Father. That's why He has placed them in a family. That's why He gives them abundance. And that's why, when you read these words, you have to ask yourself, "What is my responsibility here?" Will I be judged as a goat or a sheep—am I caring for the fatherless, or will I walk away on the other side of the street?

Chapter 9

JESUS, THE "BLESSER"

Blessed is the man
who does not walk in the counsel of the wicked
or stand in the way of sinners
or sit in the seat of mockers.

But his delight is in the law of the LORD,
and on his law he meditates day and night.

He is like a tree planted by streams of water,
which yields its fruit in season
and whose leaf does not wither.
Whatever he does prospers.

For the LORD watches over the way of the righteous,
but the way of the wicked will perish.
—Psalm 1:1–3, 6

The spring day was sunny and warm, and the boys of New Hope Centre burst out of class ready for a "tea time" snack and play time. They were full of energy that could not be contained. It was time for soccer, games, and exploring.

Springtime in Swaziland is alive with vibrant colors and lush greenery just begging the boys to run, hide, and climb the big mango tree in front of the main house. Jesse and his brothers were excitedly running in and out of the bushes on Bethany Mountain and hiding in them.

Jesse and his biological brother Noah had both become brothers to the other boys in the home when they were adopted into the Abraham family, after their mother died of cardiorespiratory failure and their father had already been confined to a hospital bed, terminally ill. When their father heard about New Hope Centre over the radio, and knew he would be unable to care for his sons, who were already living on the streets and eating grasshoppers to survive, he called the police to take us to Malkerns to locate the boys and take them to live at our home. We then went together to the hospital for the signing of the adoption papers. Jesse and Noah found a new family that day.

On this spring day, Jesse had a very important lesson to learn—a lesson of total obedience even when he didn't understand the importance of the rules. Early in the spring, the many snakes of Swaziland are waking up from their winter hibernation. They move slowly, making it dangerous to walk through tall grass or bushes. The sluggish snakes cannot quickly move away from the intruder. They are much more likely to strike and bite anyone who comes too close. The staff knew this, and had told the boys to stay out of the bushes.

Jesse didn't see any snakes and didn't see any danger. He disobeyed and went into the bushes. The worst danger is often in what you don't see, and it's important to learn obedience even when there appears to be no danger—a lesson Jesse would learn that day.

When Uncle Sabelo caught Jesse hiding in the bushes, the boy knew he was in big trouble. Jesse was frightened that a spanking was on the way, so he braced himself to be hit with a big stick. Then he heard, "Please don't hit him. Please hit me instead."

Jesse slowly opened his eyes to see Debrah, our eldest daughter, pleading to take his punishment for him. Jesse was amazed that Debrah would be willing to be punished in his place. Somehow, he knew she had a deep strength that couldn't be seen. Debrah not only spared Jesse a spanking, she reflected love in its purest form. What she did is a perfect picture of the substitutionary sacrifice Jesus made for each of us—for each of our children. He willingly paid the full price for our sins, and he said, *Greater love has no man than this, than to lay down his life for his friend* (John 15:13).

Debrah did not get punished, but she taught Jesse the greatest definition of love and the cost of disobedience.

A favorite series of books our children have learned to love is the Chronicles of Narnia. In the book *The Lion, the Witch, and the Wardrobe*, we see another picture of a sinless one sacrificed by being the substitute for someone who had done wrong.

The story happens when Edmund, the youngest boy in the Pevensie family, is enticed by the witch to betray his family. Edmund is not strong of character, and very quickly becomes a traitor to them all. All through the story, as the children wander through Narnian adventures, Edmund's heart is not with the other three children. His heart has been captured by the witch and her delicious treats. He betrays the others.

After the children have many adventures, the witch confronts Aslan the lion and says, "You have a traitor there, Aslan." Everyone knows she is speaking of Edmund. The witch reminds Aslan that there is "deep magic" with regard to Edmund's offense. The witch rages on and finally declares, "Every traitor belongs to me as my lawful prey and that for every treachery, I have a right to kill. . . . So that human creature is mine. His life is forfeit to me. His blood is my property."

Aslan tells them all that that she has said is true. A price must be paid for Edmund's betrayal. Aslan sends everyone but the witch away. The two talk and talk, and talk some more.

Finally, Aslan tells them all to come back, since he has "settled the matter."

The reader soon learns that the way the matter is "settled," is an agreement between the witch and Aslan that Aslan will die in Edmund's place—for Edmund's sin. And if you know the story, you know that is what happens. The great lion Aslan is sacrificed on a stone table for the sinner Edmund. But then soon you read about the great joy that erupts when Aslan comes back to life to live forever, and Narnia is freed of cold, winter, ice, and evil.

We, who believe in Christ, see the perfect picture of Jesus in these two stories of Narnia and Jesse. Jesus was willing to take our sins upon Himself, to die for them, to redeem us and set us free to live forever. He has provided an eternal home for us in heaven. That is the Jesus we are teaching our children about. We teach them that they are blessed by the "Blesser," Jesus. To be blessed means to be "supremely favored, blissfully happy or contented." We teach them that blessings bring happiness and thankfulness—and these are thankful children.

Let's take a closer look at what Jesus the "Blesser" taught in a sermon on a mountain in Israel.

Blessed Beyond Belief!

Blessed are they . . .

Overlooking the Sea of Galilee is a natural amphitheatre of craggy rocks and green grass. Jesus once stood here amongst a multitude of desperately eager people. They had walked for miles and gathered to hear what the Master had to share.

On this day Jesus was describing the Kingdom of Heaven—an upside-down kingdom that stood opposed to every human kingdom, to every human inclination and thought. This one speech, or message, became known as the "Beatitudes," and this discourse contains the kernels of truth that describe our children. It holds the promises in which they are destined to walk.

Blessed are the poor in spirit, for theirs is the kingdom of heaven.

He begins with *blessed are the poor in spirit.* The children who come to our home are all poor in spirit. They've all suffered abuse, be it sexual, spiritual, verbal, physical, emotional, or psychological. They've had no affirmation of their character or being. They've had no positive, loving emotional deposits made into their hearts and have little emotional strength to draw on. They've not had the Word of God spoken into them or over them. They have no earthly possessions or a place to call home, and yet, as the verse says, *theirs is the kingdom of heaven.* Even though their condition when they arrive is "poor in spirit," they have a huge promise, a true promise that will not fail them. It is that theirs is the Kingdom of Heaven. This is their inheritance. This is their true and eternal home.

This is why we work towards establishing the Kingdom of Heaven as much as possible in our home. We reflect on the protocol and ways of royalty. We take as our example the kingdom practices within Swaziland—a Kingdom nation. Here, when one is in the presence of royalty or in the royal residence, time becomes eternal. There is no hurry. No one rushes. No one scrambles. No one runs. In the presence of royalty, peace and tranquility are ever-present. So in our home, we discourage shouting or scolding one another. We encourage speech with grace, soft eyes, and soft voices. As we practice this way of life, we live out an assurance of our children's inheritance.

Blessed are those who mourn, for they will be comforted.

All of the children that come to us have had multiple bereavements. Not only have they lost one or two parents, they've lost siblings, cousins, uncles, aunts, grandparents, caregivers, and other people they trusted to take care of them. They know what mourning is, as they have witnessed funeral after funeral, loss after loss. Jesus says to them, *Blessed are those that mourn, for they shall be comforted.* The question is, who will do the comforting? Who will comfort them? The Lord Jesus, the gracious Holy Spirit, and the angels are on assignment to minister to the redeemed. Although we are there to meet them in their need, to hold them when they cry and grieve, we can only do this by His grace, by His love and by His Spirit. We try to be there for each child, but there are deep dimensions of grief that no human being can touch. They can only be addressed by the Spirit of God. The Comforter must become real to each child.

Blessed are the meek, for they shall inherit the earth.

When these children come in, they have few earthly possessions and no inheritance. Once the parents have passed away, many children have had their inheritances stolen by a relative or community member. So they have nothing at all. Even more, they are totally insignificant, overlooked, outcast, and rejected. No one has invested any time or money in them. Our children certainly come to us meek and timid. They don't feel that they own anything or have a right to anything. Little Hephzibah came some months ago; her name means "God's delight," but she was tiny, withdrawn, and forlorn. She would zone out into a blank stare, frozen in thoughts only this two-year-old knew. Now she has been with us for a while and the blank-out times are rare, the pouting is less, and the smiles and laughter have begun, as she learns that *The earth is the Lord's and everything that dwells in it,* and that this Lord is her Dad, so it all belongs to her. The Lord says that they shall inherit the earth. This is what He wants to bring to these children who are bereft of everything: He wants to bring them to full understanding of who they are in Him, and into a knowledge that all things are theirs.

Blessed are those who hunger and thirst for righteousness, for they will be filled.

When the children come to our home, most of them don't understand the word "righteousness." They don't understand if anything can be righteous to them, because they have suffered much injustice. Righteousness and justice go hand in hand. We are all made in the image of God, and in these children's spirits, they are hungry and thirsty for righteousness—and for justice. Righteousness is making things right, bringing things back into the order that God intended from the beginning of time. I believe that we each have a sense of longing for things to be right as God intended—even if all we have known is injustice. These children long for justice inside their spirits even before they come to our home. Even if they cannot articulate it, this thought is buried deep within: "Surely there is someone who will care for me," or "If there would only be someone who would care for me, then I would be fine."

And here the Word says that they shall be filled. With what? Goodness and justice. This is what New Hope Centre is all about—filling these little ones with the riches of God's goodness and righteousness. This is why we take justice so seriously in our home, even if its administration is imperfect at times. We want every child to know that he or she has been heard, and that there exists goodness and the ability to make wrongs right again. We spend a lot of time in meetings with the children, listening to their daily experiences of injustice, establishing what went wrong, and then endeavoring to overcome the wrong with wisdom, justice, and forgiveness.

Blessed are the merciful, for they shall obtain mercy.

Being merciful to others is a little more difficult to establish in our home, because when you've been abused, it's very difficult not to abuse. An abused person usually becomes an abuser. Part of the grieving process a child goes through is denial, depression, and anger that leads to social violence or bullying. Our children have experienced social violence, ridicule, bullying, stigmatism, and discrimination. It becomes a learned human behavior. Stored up inside each of them is depression, sorrow, anger, and the unfairness of everything they have lost. And it is from this well of sorrow that their abuse of others flows. They only know how to respond in the way they have been treated in the past. They have to unlearn an abusive response and learn another kinder, gentler, more gracious way to respond.

So how do you teach these battered, wounded souls about mercy? It's a slow process, but as these youngsters who know they deserve nothing begin to receive mercy, mercifulness is slowly but surely born in them. When you see little ones, like our John, taking care of other children who come in, teaching them how to do things the right way, holding a little child's hand, you see that mercy has taken hold in them. They are establishing mercy around them. Seeing little John take little Samuel to show him how to go to the toilet makes my heart leap for joy. It wasn't very long ago that John didn't know how to use the toilet himself. To see James, who is older than John, come to John for advice or to be built up in confidence—this is the blessing for those who are merciful. As soon as they receive mercy, these little ones slowly but surely become merciful.

Blessed are the pure in heart, for they shall see God.

Despite all that they come from, there is purity in the heart of a child. There is no vengeance inside these children—no right that has taken hold of them or hardened their heart. They are pure, simply seeking for someone to care for them, someone to love them. And in this verse, it is promised that they will see God.

Some take this figuratively, but our children do see God. If we were to interview each one of them, they would tell you of having seen God. They have seen Jesus face to face. It's not unusual for them. Rather, it's normal for them to see Him in their dreams at night and in their meditations in the daytime. And it's not just a glimpse of Him. They interact with Him, play soccer with Him, have birthday parties with Him, or just sit and hang out. They have seen Him.

Caleb shared that he saw Jesus coming to collect His beloved from New Hope Centre. He lifted them up into the air and they ascended into glory, each child being taken one at a time. Esther first saw Jesus while waiting on the Lord in prayer. She and Jesus were sitting at a table with a five-tiered birthday cake much like a wedding cake. The two of them were eating it and finished it all, mouthful by mouthful, giggle by giggle.

Blessed are the peacemakers, for they shall be called the sons of God.

Peace is another concept that is foreign to these children at first. When they arrive, they don't know anything about peace or making peace, but God has given us keys to working through the noise, conflict, and aggression. We use soft voices and soft eyes in dealing with the children. We also have a process of conflict resolution that involves the children, so that as they go through the process, they learn to become peacemakers.

When an offense is committed, we bring the offender and "offendee" together, as well as any witnesses of the conflict. Each has their say, and in the end they all agree on the punishment terms as well as extending forgiveness to one another. As they have more and more practice, our children are becoming the peacemakers. Caleb is already the peacemaker of the home. He volunteers himself to be the key person who handles the conflicts in the home. What young boy does that? And this has come about in only two years. Before this, he was living in the streets. As the younger ones grow and mature, they too will walk out this same gift of responding in peace when conflicts arise.

Blessed are those who are persecuted for righteousness' sake, for theirs is the kingdom of heaven.

Our children are shielded from persecution at the moment. They are in an incubator of sorts as they are growing and being nurtured by the Spirit of God. But we know that a day will come when they will leave our home and head out to the nations. As they do, they will certainly face persecutions of many kinds. There are many people who do not appreciate the love and truth for which these children stand. But as they enter into the expected persecutions, the children and the family will already know that they possess something far greater—the Kingdom of Heaven.

More Teachings from the "Blesser"

> On another day Jesus spoke, "You are the salt of the earth . . . a city on a hill . . . the light of the world."
> —Matthew 5:13–14

When we set out to build a children's home in a nation that has one of the highest HIV/AIDS rates in the world, it was clear from the beginning that we would not be able to save every orphan. On the day of our dedication, the UNICEF representative addressed the issue we are ultimately committed to caring for one hundred twenty orphans, but what about the 120,000 orphans in the nation? Much like the story of Noah in the Old Testament, we envision a remnant that will be saved, and they will be safe from the oncoming deluge. And that's why this remnant—these children—are so precious. I believe with all my heart that who they are and how they live out their lives will determine the future of this nation. They are the salt and light of Swaziland, something we reinforce again and again. We teach them that if they lose their saltiness, it will be difficult for them to be restored again after having come from the brink of death once before. We know that God is their Restorer and He is their Father. God is healing them as they grow in our home, and that gives us much hope that this remnant will do great things.

You are the light of the world.

Our house of light and hope is set on the hill and cannot be hidden. It can be seen from all over the country—from north, south, east, and west. We cannot be missed by those who pass by as we bring light to dispel darkness. As our children go out into the primary schools, preschools, and community, more and more light is established. The light of God will become known.

Let your light shine before men, for they will see your works and glorify your father in heaven.

Whenever we have a visitor at New Hope Centre, the first thing that grabs them is our children. Not literally . . . well, in some cases they are overwhelmed with the hugs and affectionate gestures. They just sense that there is something different about these children, not because of the circumstances from which they have come, but *in spite of them.* They just simply cannot imagine how children who have been raped, abused, neglected, and starved can be so full of love for strangers. It simply defies everything they have known. And so these children are not just lights in the community, but lights to everyone they encounter. And though they are still broken and bruised to some extent, they shine brightly. Indeed, it is in their brokenness that their Father is glorified, for only He can take the nothings of this world and make them into something. Only He could first love something back to life, and then, through the simple and humble love of an orphan, bring so much healing and hope to those who encounter them.

How do you know when a child has overcome? You know that children have come through the barbs and stings of their lives when they exhibit a peace, confidence, and joy that goes against all human wisdom. It's the fruit of their lives. Again and again, we see our little ones overcome and become mighty in spirit. Each child is on a different journey and timeline. Some who came in the early days are still struggling; others who have recently come are able to overcome their background speedily. And while much of their recovery happens as they relate to God, it also happens as they relate to us. That's because for many of them, adults have let them down tremendously. So sometimes we take the place of the adult who hurt them, and ask them to forgive us in the stead of that one who hurt them. Their mom may not be here anymore to say, "I am sorry," but we can stand in the gap and ask forgiveness on that mother's behalf.

Sometimes we'll call one of the big brothers or uncles to come so that the child can hear those words, "I am sorry," when the offense has come from a male. It's amazing how powerful these words can be, and how much pain and suffering they can relieve.

There is no magic to what we do. All transformations are born out of a lot of love and prayer and a huge portion of forgiveness, and once a child is able to forgive the adults who have hurt him or her by abuse, death, or neglect, that child becomes different. He or she becomes strong.

Transformation into the likeness of Jesus ultimately leads us into what we are created to be, "in the image of God, our

Creator." Our children are His triumph. The destitute of the destitute becoming the leaders of tomorrow.

So God created man in his own image, in the image of God created he him; male and female created he them.
—Genesis 1:27

But we all, with open face beholding as in a glass the glory of the Lord, are changed into the same image from glory to glory, even as by the Spirit of the Lord.
—1 Corinthians 3:18

PART IV
DAY BY DAY AND
LIFE BY LIFE

Chapter 10

DAY BY DAY AND LIFE BY LIFE

You haven't been to a birthday party until you have been
to a birthday party at New Hope Centre. There is always
a big, decorated cake that has come fresh from the bakery in
town. As mother in the home, I seek God for a verse to write
on the cake. This will be the Word from God their Father to
be established in their heart and life during the year to come.
Every member of our family prepares a handmade birthday
card for the birthday child, to express their affection and ad-
miration of the talents and gifts of the birthday child. Then,
each child stands up and speaks a blessing over the birthday
child. The birthday child of honor then stands to share with
everyone what they are thankful for in the past year, and what
they are trusting God for in the new year to come. We then
sing a blessing and share in eating the cake with much excitement and fun.

In Africa, children come last. Either by necessity or cultural
mores, there isn't a lot of hope or expectation invested in any
children—orphans even less. So you can see how something as
simple as a birthday party—a time of expectation—means the
world to a child. In a culture that doesn't give children positive

feedback, all those words of kindness from the birthday child's adopted family are better than years of therapy for building self-esteem. Most of the children come to us not even knowing the date on which they were born, so they choose a number they like, and this becomes their date of birth. So imagine the first celebration sitting in the place of honor, being blessed and loved. Some children have been overwhelmed and cried, but most are delighted, with smiles from ear to ear and sparkling, bright eyes.

There's more going on here than just honoring the birthday child. As the other children learn to stand and speak a blessing over the birthday child, they are learning a vital leadership skill—how to speak in public and express themselves. They have to give thought ahead of time to what they will say to the birthday child that will encourage him or her. They have to speak out so everyone can hear.

Why do we put all this effort, time, and resources into children who are sick, depressed, ungrateful, and perhaps even aggressive? We are doing it because these children—our children—are tomorrow's leaders, and their leadership could not come at a more crucial moment in time for Swaziland.

When God gave me the vision for New Hope Centre, He emphasized to me that it would not be an orphanage—a transitional place for hot meals and clothing and a safe place to sleep. He gave me the vision that it would be a home, and it would house the leaders of tomorrow. We would raise children who would win Olympic gold medals and become prime ministers, bankers, teachers, missionaries, pastors, nurses, doctors, lawyers, and judges. All their destinies, while different, would be connected by the thread of leadership. And so, at our home, we invest in leadership training based on Jesus' character traits, because it is an investment that will not only benefit the children, but the entire nation of Swaziland and the continent of Africa.

We think of AIDS as stealing away people's lives, but it is more than that. AIDS is the biggest robber of legacy. It takes people in the prime of life. It steals away primary caregivers, teachers, and leaders in one fell swoop. In other words, it takes those who should be passing on values and family history and all the things young children should be learning in a family setting. They have no legacy. And while we are unable to take in all the orphans in the country, our mandate from the beginning has been to save a remnant and invest our everything in them. It is the principle of multiplication—of compounded interest. We invest in one child who invests in two children, who invest in four children, and on and on until thousands throughout the nation are reached and helped. What we invest in these children now will pay dividends down the road. And in Swaziland, with one of the highest HIV/AIDS rates in the world, there is no hope for the nation unless this remnant is saved and preserved. So everything we do is done with this focus in mind.

It Starts with the ABC's

When we first opened New Hope Centre, we started by sending our children to schools in the area. But because we live on the top of a rural mountain, the journey was long for the children. They had to leave home at 6 A.M. and return late in the afternoon carrying heavy book bags up the hill. We also learned that school can be a hazardous place for orphans. Ask any teacher who the problem child is in their classroom, and they will tell you it's an orphan. They are at the centre of any disruption, school brawl, or classroom antics. This is not because they are naughty; it is because they are carrying a heavy load of unresolved anger and don't know what to do with it. Their anger erupts when they are teased or marginalized because of their orphan status, which is considered shameful in Swazi culture, as they are fatherless. Often, because of their harsh life circumstances, they are behind in school, and that only makes them more of a target for ridicule and discrimination.

When the children come to us, they are already beaten down, and many of them—even those as old as eight or nine—are still illiterate. So in educating them, we have to find a way to coax them gently into learning, while at the same time rebuilding their trust in themselves and in authority figures.

The School of the Happy Overcomers

My niece, Tracie, was in England when we started New Hope Centre. She and her friend were preparing to buy a preschool centre and run it as a business. Although she was young, she had a dream, and was making headway toward that dream when God touched her heart for Swaziland. At twenty years of age, she left home, family, and friends and came to help out. She found herself establishing a preschool at New Hope Centre for our orphan children and the children of the community around us.

We knew that we wanted to use a Christian educational model to teach the children. They needed just as much spiritual training as academic training. Tracie looked around for a suitable curriculum and discovered nothing that fit the uniqueness of our situation. Imagine an eight-year-old child who can't even hold a pen, let alone write his name. And yet, thrusting such a child into a primary school program would only cause more shame and anger which would overwhelm the child.

This is how the School of the Happy Overcomers was born. Here is a place where children of any age can play and heal until they are ready to tackle primary school. We also decided that our school would not just be for our own children, but also children in the outlying community of Bethany. It's a community sick with AIDS, poverty, unemployment, and witchcraft. We decided to see what schools were charging for fees, and set our fee at a nominal amount of $12 (U.S.) a month. Fifty percent of our preschoolers are from the community. The preschool curriculum is based on each book of the Old Testament, the Gospels, and the Epistles, and gives them piece by piece the tools they need to grow in wisdom, understanding, and self-esteem.

In most cases, not much learning takes place during the first six months. The children just need to cry and get their anger out. When the anger is finally on the outside, they are able to begin learning. As they start to learn right from wrong, they begin to teach others in the class and in the community. Tracie has seen some of the worst-behaved children become the best helpers. Young Ethan came to us carrying a load of destructive anger inside him. He would hit other children or adults and seemed unreachable. He trusted no adults and had no regard for siblings. One day, Tracie gave him some drum sticks and an empty five-liter paint tin. We told him to hit the tin until he was finished being angry. For about three weeks he beat the tin daily, until one day he came to Tracie and said, "You can have back the tin, I don't need this now." He has not beaten up anyone since—what a breakthrough!

Before children can ever lead and grow, they need to know who they are. They need to know to whom they belong, and that they matter. Self-esteem and encouragement are the building blocks of leadership training in preschool. That's why we start their training with Genesis. "In the beginning" establishes that they are made in the image of God. They are His crowning creation. They are no mistake, but precious and special in the earth.

Tracie took the early childhood learning goals for pre-school—social, emotional, physical, creativity, mathematics knowledge, understanding of the world, language, and literacy development—and fleshed them out, using the Bible from Genesis through to the Epistles as the basis for the curriculum. It was quite a challenge to develop the curriculum, but it has become a rich teaching tool.

The first term begins with the creation story, teaching the children they were created by God and that no witch doctor made them. They learn not only that God made them, but also that He made everything around them. They learn about colors and how plants grow. They interact with creation by planting their own flowers. They learn about weather cycles through the story of Noah's ark, as well as the consequences of obedience and disobedience.

The second term begins with Passover, the Exodus from Egypt with the evidence of God's miraculous intervention for the deliverance of the nation of Israel, following on to the wondrous work of Jesus on the cross. He was our Passover lamb, sacrificed for our guilt, shame, pain, and sorrow to deliver us into life, joy, acceptance, and hope.

Then we move on to the Ten Commandments, handed down from God to Moses on Mount Sinai. On our mountain, there is a prevalence of witchcraft and sexual abuse; not exactly standard preschool subject matter, but by three years of age, many of the children from the community know all the terms already. Sadly, many have been sexually abused. They even reenact rape scenes as they play with dolls in school. So Tracie spends a week teaching the subject of sexuality, using the commandment, "Don't commit adultery." Starting with drawings of their bodies, they learn the difference between appropriate and inappropriate touch. This can be the first point in healing for many of them.

Idolatry is another subject that is foreign to most preschool curriculums. However, witchcraft is a reality in Swaziland. Many children have been offered over the fire to their ancestral spirits. Many children have also been taken to witch doctors and have had their bodies mutilated, either to release "bad" spirits or to insert herbs, ashes, and bits of wood or bone to "empower" the child. Some people have expressed anger at us for teaching against these practices, since it is part of the

Swazi culture. So to be certain that parents understand what will be taught, each year we send a letter home with the child emphasizing that we are a "Christian" school and we believe that there is only one God. So far, no parent has removed a child over this matter.

The term continues through the celebration of Pentecost, when the Holy Spirit came down. We want the children to grow the fruit of the Spirit in their personal lives. The teaching on love, joy, peace, patience, faithfulness, gentleness, goodness, kindness, and self control brings us into the themes of Christ. They learn of the gifts of the Spirit empowering them to do the works of Jesus through healing, miracles, faith, speaking in tongues, interpreting tongues, words of wisdom, words of knowledge, prophecy, and discerning spirits. We end the term with a study on the armor of God—what it is, and how to wear and use it effectively in their lives. We teach them about the helmet of salvation that brings their minds, attitudes, and thoughts into the will of God concerning them. The breast-plate of righteousness is given to keep condemnation and guilt far away, through living right and being cleansed by the blood of Jesus when we slip or fall spiritually. The shoes of peace protect our feet as we walk in the footsteps of Jesus. The belt of truth gives us the strength of integrity and a clear conscience. The shield of faith deflects the accusing thoughts and words around us. And the sword of the Spirit is the Word of God, that they can wield to open the way forward in their lives. Putting on the full armor of God helps our child to establish health, wealth, success, integrity, peace, renewed strength, joy, and a host of other spiritual benefits in their lives.

As the preschoolers make their way through the term, they get into the inspirational stories of the Bible. They love the story of David and Goliath because it shows them that God can use young people in a mighty way.

The last term is spent learning about Jesus, starting with His birth, then moving on to Him as a young boy teaching in the tabernacle. The children learn that they, too, can teach at a young age as Jesus did. They learn the healing stories of Jesus—that He can heal them and that, through them, others can be healed.

We go through how Jesus died for us, and what it means. We learn about the disciples and the others Jesus had with Him so that He could teach them. The children know the Bible. They know who wrote it. They draw pictures about the stories. They learn that they can have a relationship with Jesus. They learn how wonderful Jesus is today. By the time the term ends with Christmas celebrations, they know why the whole world celebrates Christmas. They understand that Jesus truly deserves to be honored with a worldwide public holiday and parties, picnics (in the Southern Hemisphere), and turkey or chicken dinners.

As a family, we do a lot of waiting on God. We sit together and pray and ask the Lord to be with us. We close our eyes and ask Him if He would like to show us anything for the day. We wait for three minutes, and when the time is up, we open our eyes. If the children want to, they can share something that has been impressed upon their mind and heart. They all like to share what Jesus has shown them. One child may say, "Jesus told me I must be good," and another says that she was on the swing with Him. Others play football with Him, and still others share a birthday cake with Him. Esther shared recently that God told her that because she has been faithful in using her gift of healing and praying for the sick, now God was releasing to her the authority to raise the dead. They learn that they can have relationship with Jesus and can talk to Him. By the time they reach this point, they are different children from those who first came to us. Sometimes they have travelled in the spirit realm with Jesus, seeing things not usually seen or known.

Rewards

We have a reward chart where we place stars at the end of the day. The children become the judges. It is they who evaluate the behavior of others. They say why someone is a star and another is not. This is how they learn right from wrong, and good behavior from bad. Once a child gets ten stars, he or she can choose a reward from a grab-bag of donated supplies.

By this constant encouragement, even the preschoolers who come from the community are turning into little leaders. Many of those community children are also missing a parent. Or they may be living with a relative who just doesn't have the ability to invest in their lives. But these little ones take what they have learned into their homes. They go out from our preschool as beacons of light in a sea of darkness.

Once our own children complete the preschool process, it's time to tackle primary school. Again, there are some unique challenges in educating orphans of such diverse ages and backgrounds. Putting them in grades by age was out of the question, as many eight- or nine-year-olds were still illiterate, and some younger ones had received only a little education prior to their arrival here. We didn't want to create a competitive classroom atmosphere where their performance would be constantly judged and compared to that of others.

The community children who moved on from our preschool into the public schools have excelled, and reports come in regularly of how the graduates of the School of the Happy Overcomers have excelled academically, socially, artistically, and linguistically, and shine brightly in their success and achievements.

Accelerated Christian Education

As we thought and prayed, the pieces fell into place. We found the internationally recognized Accelerated Christian

Education (ACE) program, that had originally been designed for missionary children who are often in remote places and have to learn on their own. All children start at the same level, but depending on their motivation, they can work their way up fast, sometimes accomplishing two grades in a year.

The program is based on sixty character traits of Jesus. He is the greatest leader of all time. As the children learn the alphabet, they are introduced to the character traits of Jesus. For example: A is for "Ape," and the characteristic is "consideration." Soft "a" is for "antelope," and the characteristic is "discreet." "E" is for "Emu," "a merciful creature." At each level, the character is reinforced through stories about the animal. The children don't just learn the trait, they also incorporate and interact with that trait through stories and activities with the hope that they will internalize the trait before they move on to the next level. By the time they've learned their ABC's, they have learned both the alphabet and phonics, together with the character traits of Jesus.

Character is crucial if our children are to be leaders. This must be instilled in them while they are young. In this program, they have to take responsibility for their own education, their own pace of study and standard of accomplishment, and that too builds self-esteem.

The onus of learning isn't on the teacher, but on the student. Their progress is based on how hard they are willing to work and learn. We are blessed to have a dedicated educational supervisor, Miss Thandi, who has helped them not only learn how to read and write, but to become children of character—leaders of tomorrow. It is our firm belief that we should *train a child in the way she should go, and he will not turn from it* (Prov. 22:6).

Our whole purpose in the way we teach our children is self-actualization (becoming who they were designed or created to be), but also to be Christ to others. They are to become His emissaries on earth. We are investing in every way to give them the opportunity and ingredients that will enable them to live out His purpose for their lives.

Towards this end, we make every effort to enable our children to remain close to the communities, schools, and circumstances from which they came. As they learn and grow their skills as leaders, they will impact the nation's survival through this AIDS pandemic, starting with peer education. There is something powerful about children teaching children. So whenever we get the opportunity, we go to schools across the country doing skits, teaching on the basics of hygiene and personal care, as well as imparting scripture and blessings to those we encounter. When school children see children from the most destitute of circumstances take up the leadership mantle and care for others, it communicates that there is hope for them as well.

As a family, we go out to the community homesteads once a month. Jesus talked about feeding Him when He was hungry, clothing Him when He was naked, and visiting Him when he was sick or in prison. *Jesus said, "When you do it unto the least of these you do it unto me"* (Matt. 25:40). So in keeping with caring for Jesus, we share the abundance that comes our way, whether it is yogurt, potatoes, or even flip flops. We visit the children's ward in the RFM Hospital nearby. After the children deliver their gifts and see the faces of those who receive the gifts light up with smiles, the leader of the group offers a spiritual blessing over the child in the hospital bed. The children read scripture, give a brief teaching, and then pray. We love it when friends have brought in an abundance of teddy bears that we can give. Every child around the world, and especially in a hospital room far away from home, loves to cuddle a soft, fuzzy teddy bear. We have obtained the special privilege of visiting the prisons and correctional services in Swaziland, bringing a message of hope, joy, and forgiveness through Christ. Recently, we visited the inmates of the maximum security prison. What an amazing experience to see the softness and gentleness in the eyes of hardened men while children ministered through songs and dramas, or through serving them a huge piece of cake or a cup of juice. All of this is a part of learning to live life and to have life even more abundantly. As our children grow and develop, we know their ministry in the community will be great as they go from strength to strength.

We want our whole mountain to be filled with the knowledge of the glory and goodness of God. And our young leaders are just the ones to do the job. Like light radiating from a candle on a hill, these precious young lives are already impacting the nation in ever-increasing circles, bringing hope and a lively expectation that God is a Father who cares and is ready, willing, and able to intervene practically and miraculously in every person's life.

Chapel and Devotions

Every morning at eight, as soon as chores are finished, the whole family—adults and children—have chapel. This is a time of praise and worship and dancing together. Children from the community who attend our school are there to participate as well. Then one of the family—either an adult or a child—takes a turn and shares the Word of God. That person selects songs and a memory verse that reinforce a central theme. Then he or she leads everyone in prayer.

On Saturday mornings, we don't have praise and worship time because we celebrate *Shabbat* the night before. So, we spend time waiting on the Lord in small groups to hear what He wants to share with us. This is often a time where many of our children have visions. It is at this time that some of them receive healing in their hearts and minds.

In the evenings, our devotions involve praise and worship followed by a teaching time with the children. We don't just read the Bible; we study it and encourage activities that will help the children internalize the message. First, they take a Bible character or story and meditate on it and ask what they need God to do in them, and what they need God to take out of them, so that they can live out what they have just read or studied.

For example, after reading the story of Daniel and the lion's den, a child may ask, "What in me needs to be removed so that I can be in a cave full of lions and still trust God my Father to protect me? What must come out of me? Fear? Distrust? Uncertainty of the will of God concerning my life? What would it take to make me ready to go boldly into a cave of hungry lions and not be fearful?" Second, they ask, "What do I need to put into me so that I can do this?" So we focus on scriptures that talk about courage and strength, trust and confidence.

Every afternoon at 4 P.M. we take thirty minutes for a time of thanksgiving. This is so that every day the Lord can look down at this hill in Bethany that is our home and hear His little children say what they are thankful for that day. We encourage them to be thankful not just for general things, but for specifics. Before they go to playtime, we encourage them to identify precisely what they need to thank God for, what they need to thank their Savior for, and what they need to thank the Holy Spirit for. One visitor to the home was deeply touched as Debrah thanked God for life itself. While it was seemingly a simple thanksgiving, to the visitor it meant much more. The other volunteers and the children did not know that she was a cancer survivor. She knew that it was only through God's grace and healing power that she was sitting here listening to the children give thanks to God for life.

Shabbat

Friday afternoons are a highlight of the week. School is shut down, and our children have no chores, just play. By six o'clock, everyone is in good spirits as we prepare for Shabbat. Some people find it peculiar that we celebrate a Jewish holiday, but we believe in honoring the Jewish roots of our faith. The Bible is clear about honoring the Sabbath and keeping it holy (Lev. 23:2–3; Deut. 5:12–15; Exod. 20:8–11; Mark 2:27–28). So we do. Once the table is set for the evening meal, the bread and wine symbols are put in place, and a scrumptious dinner—the best meal of the week—is ready, we begin. The mother of the house starts the evening by lighting two candles. One represents Jesus, the Light of the World, and the second represents us, as we become the light of the world through *Yeshua* (Jesus) shining out through us. As Jesus brought light, He dispelled fear, confusion, and darkness. Jesus brought understanding and revelation that brings peace, healing, and confidence. The candles burn throughout the evening until everything is finished.

This part of the ceremony is followed by the father (perhaps a boy or an uncle) standing up and speaking a blessing over the family, as would be done by the father in a Jewish home. He blesses the mother first, and then the rest of the family by going around the room laying hands on each family member and speaking a blessing directly into their life. The whole family then raises their hands and speaks blessings over the father of the home. They bless him with fruits of the Spirit and the spiritual blessings he needs. Following that, we share from the Word of God and remind each other that it is by the application of God's Word to our lives that we are strengthened in our spirits. Following that, we share the bread and wine together. Each week, different children, volunteers, or workers will bless and break the bread. As the children receive the emblems of Christ's broken body, they thank Jesus that it is by the stripes that Jesus bore in His body that we are healed (Isa. 53:5; 1 Pet. 2:24). At times, we might use another concept, and speak a special Word into ourselves as we symbolically "chew" on the Word of God. We take the cup of grape juice and bless it, then share it around the room, celebrating the blood of Jesus which has taken away all our sins, sickness, pains, and sorrows. It is the cup of joy. Finally, we take salt and dip a finger in it and declare that we are the salt of the earth. When we're finished, we give a psalm of thanksgiving and eat the meal.

After supper and after we clear the dishes, we have a feast of the Word of God. Each child prepares to give a verse or chapter that they have memorized. They recite in front of everyone, and if they pass the memory test, they earn a reward. They earn one lilangeni for a verse they have memorized, and ten emalangeni for a chapter. When they speak, we expect them to stand tall with two feet on the floor and hands at their sides, and to speak loudly enough that a person at the back of the room can hear them. Often, a child may go blank, even if he or she knows the verse, so the children help one another practice before the big night so they can be successful in their recitation.

We want to inspire them to learn entire books of the Bible. They are challenged to memorize Psalms, Proverbs, Matthew, and Acts, and after that to go on to Revelation, Isaiah, Ezekiel, and Genesis. It's a tall order, but we want to give the children the opportunity to achieve memorization of scripture. Hiding God's Word in their hearts is the best way to keep them on the path that leads to heaven, and gives them the tools needed to live an overcoming life. *Thy word is a lamp unto my feet and a light unto my path* (Ps. 119:105).

The Feasts

Our entire year is a time of celebration. We celebrate everything. When God brought the Children of Israel out of Egypt, He put them through many experiences. It was His way of training them to become a nation, rather than the ragtag mob of slaves that journeyed out of Egypt. These people were descendents of Abraham. They were the chosen ones—God's children. But they hadn't formed a national identity and a unique way of life.

So when God called them out of Egypt and to Himself, He shared with Moses the statutes and laws that were to be embraced by the people as they established their nationhood and cultural character. As we study the biblical feasts of the year, the Lord reveals Himself and His ways to us through these celebrations. That's why we celebrate Shabbat every week. It is our way of honoring God as our creator. He worked for six days, and on the seventh, He rested. So on Friday night we celebrate completing the six days of work, and on Saturday, the seventh day, we rest.

And the Lord spoke to Moses saying,

"Speak to the children of Israel, and say to them: 'The feasts of the Lord, which you shall proclaim to be holy convocations, these are My feasts. Six days shall work be done, but the seventh day is a Sabbath of solemn rest, a holy convocation. You shall do no work on it; it is the Sabbath of the Lord in all your dwellings. These are the feasts of the Lord, holy convocations which you shall proclaim at their appointed times.'"
—Leviticus 23:1–4

Three times a year all your males shall appear before the Lord your God in the place which He chooses: at the Feast of Unleavened Bread, at the Feast of Weeks, and at the Feast of Tabernacles; and they shall not appear before the Lord empty-handed.
—Deuteronomy 16:16–17

Seven Feasts We Celebrate

The Lord gave seven ordinances for His people to celebrate in seasons so that we would understand the heart, the ways, and the purposes of God in our lives. The first ordinance was the celebration of Shabbat, which we follow each week, honoring the six days our creator used to complete His wondrous work, and the seventh day, on which He rested. In Leviticus 23, we find the other ordinances well described and defined: Passover, Unleavened Bread, Feast of Weeks, Rosh HaShanah, Feast of Tabernacles, and Trumpets, the three high Feasts, every Israelite was required to come up to Jerusalem to celebrate, and in the Feast of Tabernacles, all foreigners were invited to participate in Jerusalem.

The preschool curriculum follows this annual calendar, revealing the meaning and importance of each of these Feasts of the Lord. We celebrate these as a family, and also include Purim (Esther's salvation), Hannukah (the Festival of Lights), and Christmas (Jesus' birthday). Each of the Feasts has historic and prophetic components that are important in order to keep before us the nature of the Lord our God, Yahweh (Jehovah). *Jesus said, "I do always those things that please the Father"* (John 8:29), so we are to be like Jesus and do the ordinances that please the Father.

Passover (Pasach)

We celebrate the passover in conjunction with the fulfillment of the prophetic events in the trial, crucifixion, burial, and resurrection of Christ Jesus.

Thursday night, we celebrate the Passover by making unleavened bread, barbequing the lamb, and preparing the tables and plates in the traditional way to remember the deliverance of Israel from slavery in Egypt. We follow the Seder meal, with connections to the meaning in the deliverance of each of us from sin to glorious life in Christ Jesus. This is a very formal meal, plentiful in all aspects, and is celebrated in place of Shabbat for that week.

Special preparations include:

- Apples
- Cinnamon
- Horse radish
- Parsley
- Lamb shoulder cuts with piece of bone—large slices, one per person (Uncles' braai—barbequed meat)
- Boiled eggs
- Unleavened bread (thin pancakes), plus matzoz
- Specially prepared tables and plates
- Four wine glasses (filled with grape juice)
- Two Shabbat candles

On Good Friday, we fast from after breakfast until 3 P.M., when Jesus declared, "It is finished." We watch portions of *The Passion of the Christ* by Mel Gibson, reflecting on the suffering and price paid for each of us, and the tremendous love that took our place, our pain, our sin, our sickness, and our death. We meditate particularly on the seven wounds of Christ:

1. Drops of blood in Gethsemane (stress in conflict—Thy will be done);
2. Facial hair pulled out (shame); bruises from rough handling (iniquities);
3. Crown of thorns on His head. "This Is Christ the King of the Jews" (for the redemption of our souls, thoughts to be renewed by His Word);
4. The thirty-nine stripes furrowing His body (healing of our suffering, pain, sickness, disease, and infirmities);
5. Nails in His hands (redemption of the works of our hands, our sins of commission and omission empowering us to bless, prosper, and heal by the laying on of hands);

6. Nails in His feet (redemption of the sins we collect by walking and living in this world, to be in the world and not of this world, living the gospel of peace wherever we walk with our feet, making our feet beautiful on the mountains as we bring good news, claiming the land and the earth back into the dominion of the Kingdom of God);
7. Pierced side from where His heart was pierced flowing with blood and water (for the purity of heart redeeming our hearts of wickedness, *Blessed are the pure in heart for they shall see God*).

At 3 P.M., we finish, and enjoy sweet tea and hot cross buns before heading up to the mountain to pray for the nation—the Kingdom of Swaziland—making declarations from the scriptures, and prophecies relating to the divine destiny and purpose of this nation.

On Saturday, we spend the morning visiting the Stations of the Cross, meditating on the fourteen Stations of the Cross in order to bring us each to a place of introspection until noontime. Then we celebrate that Jesus is winning victory for us in all of these areas—He was in hell taking the keys of the Kingdom from the devil, reclaiming the rights and authority for us to rule and reign once more upon the earth, and emptying Hell and Hades. Lunch is a party of candy, cakes, popcorn, chips, and all sorts of party foods that we don't usually eat, including ice cream and all things nice. In the evening, we watch a video of *The Ten Commandments* together as a family, and eat peanuts.

Sunday, we celebrate Resurrection Day with King Mswati III and the nation of Swaziland at the Somhlolo National Stadium. It is a long service. We leave at 8 A.M. in order to get into the stadium safely and have seats under the bleachers before the crowds arrive. We take with us water and "teatime" snacks of peanut butter sandwiches, and bologna and mayonnaise sandwiches and juice for lunch. We usually get home at about 3 P.M.

Monday is a public holiday to rest, go on hikes, swim, or visit the game park, which is something special and free.

Pentecost (Feast of Weeks)

We begin celebrating with the preschool parents and students with a Pentecost party. This is the day that the Lord gave His Word and married Israel at Mount Sinai. This is the day the Lord gave His Spirit to write His word in our hearts at Mount Zion. We have a drama presented by the preschool, and a party with the parents. Then every family is given two loaves of sweet bread, symbolizing that the nation of Israel and the nation of the church of Jesus Christ are of one substance, though one is Hebrew and the other is Gentile. The preschoolers all take home their two loaves to share with their families. The preschoolers make hats with "tongues of fire," and scrolls with the Word of God written on them, worn on their hearts.

We celebrate Shabbat wearing red, orange, and yellow, for the flames of the Holy Spirit. We have a barbecue with plenty of meat and pap—traditional porridge made from mielie-meal (ground maize or other grain), and we light fires in nine drums to represent the nine gifts of the Holy Spirit. As we declare each gift, we pour oil onto the flames as a symbol that it is our duty to "fan" the flames of the anointing and power of the gifts to be used to bring the reality of the gospel into the lives of everyone we meet. On this day, we all receive gifts of shoes and any other new blessings we have, like sweaters, uniforms, or fleeces, as we prepare for winter. We give and receive as a symbol that it is the time that God gave His Word, His Son, (the Word made flesh) and the Holy Spirit.

Three spring Feasts were fulfilled in Jesus' first coming, and the three fall Feasts are prophetic of His second coming that is yet to be fulfilled.

Rosh HaShanah and the Feast of Tabernacles

Leviticus 23:24—the first day of the seventh month, the Shabbat month, Jesus' second coming in the fall feast not yet fulfilled, but we celebrate in anticipation of the faithfulness of God as we enter the promised land of the goodness of God.

It is our hope and commitment to have some Swazis in Jerusalem every year for the Feast of Tabernacles, as a prophetic declaration of the end times when all nations will be required to come up to Zion for this Feast. We pray and prepare for four children to go each year who are ready to be baptized in water, making an outward demonstration of their inward choice to serve the Lord and love Him with all their heart, all their soul, and all their strength. It is our hope that each one will be able to go to the Feast while they are living at New Hope Centre, and that they will be baptized in the River Jordan.

Those at home celebrate Rosh HaShanah on the Shabbat before the feast. The uncles prepare the materials for building the family *succah,* and the whole family works together on Friday afternoon to put up the *succah*. We celebrate this Shabbat under the stars (provided it does not rain), and we declare the Word of the Lord for the new spiritual year, eating honey and apples. We make this declaration: "God is going to pour His goodness over my life in this year, like great drops of honey." The rest of the week, we eat lunch and supper under the *succah* and under the stars, symbolizing the amazing protection and provision God gave the children of Israel in the wilderness, and His wonderful provision for each of us every day.

The last Shabbat of the Feast is the celebration of Trumpets, and all of us wear gold and/or white clothes. We have a barbeque of plenty, the children decorate the *succah* with pictures of fruits, and we tie up in the *succah* an abundance of fresh fruits for all to eat with supper.

Hannukah (Festival of Lights)

This is the week of remembrance of the miracle of light, when God multiplied the oil of one day to cover the seven days needed to prepare the oil for perpetual flame in the temple. We meet at 6 P.M. outside around the menorah and we light the first candle the first day, two candles the second day, etc. We have praise and worship for twenty to thirty minutes and read the scripture together while the candle burns, before we go in and have supper as usual.

Christmas Is Jesus' Birthday

All of our children have arbitrarily-selected birthdays because few of them know their real date of birth. So it is easy to understand that this is a day chosen to celebrate Jesus' birthday, though it may not be the real day. It is not an ordinance, but it is our way of giving thanks for the gift of life given when Jesus was born and the Word became flesh and dwelt amongst us.

We begin preparing for this day with the first Shabbat of Advent. Each night of the first week, we light the first candle and read the scriptures related to the meaning of the first candle prophecy; the second week, two candles; the third week, three candles; and the fourth week, four candles, reading and explaining and praying into being the scriptures of each day to prepare our hearts for King Jesus' birthday.

Each year, we have been given extra money to celebrate Christmas by kind, generous, thoughtful individuals. We spend days preparing the food for Christmas dinner, which we eat on Christmas Eve night before we spend the evening retelling in drama and song the story of Jesus' birth, and then singing traditional carols until midnight. At midnight, we light the Jesus candles and then open our gifts. We try to prepare a minimum of five gifts for each child of new clothes or toys or something new, so that everyone has five, the number of grace, for this day is in honor of great grace.

Christmas morning, we are up early to go to the Anglican cathedral in Mbabane for the high Mass. The children are prepared and practiced to take communion formally in church; they know the scriptures of the liturgy from memory and participate fully in the service. The rest of the day is free for fun in the sun.

New Years' Eve Is Oscar night

After supper, we gather to complete the "Altar of Thanksgiving," where we pin onto the altar banner the picture, the word, or the scripture that represents what we are most thankful for in the year that is ending. This we have been preparing in the week following Christmas. We then establish an altar of prophetic word that we have prepared in anticipation of our focus for the incoming year.

Then we have the fun of the Oscars—we prepare skits, songs, and games to be done between the Oscar awards, for the different character traits of Jesus, and the different children that need to be honored. It is a night of fun and laughter, led by one of the girls and one of the boys in the family.

Purim (Esther's Deliverance)

We celebrate this feast early in the year, with Esther as the lead role in the drama. We invite all the Jewish families in Swaziland and have a fun picnic day of drama, lunch, and games. Everyone is dressed up in costumes to celebrate the day that Esther, an orphan girl, saved the nation of Israel, prophetically celebrating the destiny of this family by raising up the standard of love and mercy in the hour of the flood of death, disease, and despair.

Sunday

Each and every week, on the first day of the week, we go to church together. This is the day to celebrate the resurrection of Jesus. We often focus on His death for the penalty of our sins, or His blood, which cleanses us and makes us pure, but we want to celebrate with body, soul, and spirit His resurrection, which is our eternal hope of glory. A day is coming when in a twinkling of an eye every one of us, living or asleep in the ground, will experience this resurrection power, this transformation into His likeness in glorified bodies. We attend a church in Manzini called "The Sword and Spirit Church." The people there have accepted us and made us feel valuable. We are invited to give a song or dance, or to share a scripture. The sharing causes the children to feel that they are making an important contribution. The pastor is a man of God who spends much time in prayer and with the Holy Spirit. His sermons are fresh and full of spiritual life.

One of our children, Lydia, went to counseling, and was asked to draw her home. She drew a big house and a small house. The big one, she explained, was New Hope Centre. "That's where my family lives," she said. Then the counselor pointed to the smaller one. "That is the Sword and Spirit Church. It is my church. It is smaller because we only go there one day a week." And that's exactly what the church is supposed to be. It is part and parcel of the fabric of our family's life.

On two different occasions, the church arranged for national Swazi TV to come to our home and videotape our Christmas drama. It was later aired all over the country. More recently, we did another video, which is called "The Swazi Dream." It too has aired throughout the country on national television.

This is a snapshot of the bustling, happy home on Bethany Mountain, Swaziland. We are proud of what God is doing in the lives of our children. We know there is more to come—much more that will come with time.

Chapter 11

LIFE IN A WOODEN ARK

Have you ever given any thought to what life was life on the ark? One thing for sure—there was a lot of *life* going on in the ark. Animals ate, slept, and did what animals do, leaving the residue for Noah and his sons to shovel out of the ark. It's pretty certain that after a few days on the boat, Noah and his family settled into a routine: wake up, feed the animals, clean up after them, take a nap, wake up, feed the animals, clean up after them, and get ready for bed.

The ark was filled with life and all that is required to maintain life. Our home—our own ark, here on a mountaintop in Swaziland—is teeming with life, and we have to have routine and training so that we can accomplish what needs to be done to maintain life here. It's a growing process that is dictated by need and by what we want to accomplish in the lives of these young people.

When God created the earth, He didn't do it all at once. Every day, something new came into existence. One by one, the pieces were fitted into the giant, intricate puzzle of life. There was a natural order to what God did. His final creative work was man. We are, by far, the most complex of His creation, bearing His image within us. But even within His creation, there are cycles of life and death, beginnings and endings and then, miraculously, new beginnings again, and so it is with our children. As they grow and learn and change, they are soon very different people from who they were when they first arrived at our home.

When these broken children arrive, they are in the worst emotional state imaginable. They are full of inexplicable trauma. We know that, and for that reason we do not force the children to tell their stories. Their stories of trouble and trauma must come in the fullness of time—when they are ready. Telling their stories is something they can only do with the help of the Holy Spirit.

We thank God daily for the Holy Spirit. He is the Helper. He is the Comforter. It is He who quickens the Word of God in our children's hearts. Many people are familiar with Jesus. They know Him either as a teacher, prophet, all-around good guy, or, for Christians, the Savior of the world. Most people are familiar with God the Father, but when talk turns to the third Person of the Trinity, the Holy Spirit, there are several reactions, ranging from fear of a spooky ghost, to indifference, to lack of understanding of the Holy Spirit's function and purpose. Many Christians downplay the importance of the Holy Spirit's activity in our lives today. They read in the Bible that the Holy Spirit came to the believers of the early church who were gathered in an upper room in Jerusalem. They acknowledge that there was wind and fire and the believers spoke in "tongues" (languages) they had not learned, but they believe that those miracles of the Holy Spirit were for the early church and are not operational today.

At our home, we could not manage without the Holy Spirit active and present in every part of our day. He is the mighty Counselor—He guides us into all truth. He is the One who speaks only what He hears from the Father, and who tells us what is to come. He is the One who makes known to us the mind and character of God. And that's why we follow His cues when it comes to unlocking the grief and trauma that is within each child. When the Holy Spirit gives us the key to the trauma and sorrow these little ones have suffered, then healing can begin. But there is healing of another kind. It is the healing that comes through learning and performing routine tasks of life. It's what we call "healing through everyday living."

Meeting the Basic Needs

We've already talked in another chapter about Maslow's hierarchy of needs, where the needs of individuals are stacked one on top of another and the individual works his way up through the layers to a place of self-actualization, starting with having physiological needs met, safety, love and belonging, esteem to self-actualization. In spiritual terms, self-actualization would be fulfilling your destiny—doing what you were created to do. It is life when everything is operating at full capacity. We believe we are watching God take these children from a place where they didn't have an identity, or even their most basic needs met, right up to the privileged summit that few people ever reach—self-actualization.

There are thousands of children throughout Swaziland, and thousands upon thousands more in Africa and around the world, that don't have the most basic physiological needs of water and food. Our children were found and brought to New Hope Centre where we started them on their climb up the pyramid to self-actualization by providing them with water, nutritious food (vegetables and fruit from our garden), and vitamins which help strengthen them and give them an appetite. (A ministry called Manna Relief donates vitamins to us, enabling our children to have a stronger immune system and helping to repair their ravaged skin.) The children are responsible for cultivating the gardens that not only provide them with nutritious food, but give them the honor of being a provider of basic necessities for our home. By tending the gardens and fruit trees, they are giving back to the home, and that is important for their sense of dignity and self-esteem.

Our children are more than just providers for the home. They are also caretakers. This is where routine is vital. You won't meet many children who like to do chores, but chores are a way of life and children learn much by taking care of their surroundings. Each task is rotated, so that no child is stuck doing one particular chore endlessly. Because we are limited in resources and manpower, we could not possibly cook, clean, and care for the emotional, physical, and spiritual needs of so many children. It's more than just assigning chores to get the work done. We are teaching them how to care for themselves and others. In most African homes, children bear a heavy load of chores, and often, an orphan bears even more since they are passed around from relative to relative.

Routine Is Not Routine—It Is Establishing the Kingdom of Heaven

Our day begins at 6 A.M. every weekday morning with the blowing of the *shofar*—a ram's horn that was used by ancient Israelites to announce the sons of God coming forth for the day. Since our children are the sons and daughters of God, we think this is an appropriate way to awaken them, rather than by the use of an alarm clock. The children all call, "Come joy, come Spirit of joy," because the joy of the Lord is our strength. We also teach our children to pray for the peace of Jerusalem because the Lord promises that when they do, they will prosper, and we want our children to prosper.

Pray for the peace of Jerusalem; "May they prosper who love you."

—Psalm 122:6

Hygiene

Hygiene is a big part of the children's daily routine. We hope to instill in them a sense of self-care as well as preventing them from getting infections and illnesses. Personal hygiene is a challenge for these children. When the children arrive, some of them have only been bathed once in their lives. And by "bathed," I mean they were washed in a bucket or dunked in the river. A couple of children said that the only times they were washed was by going to the river where a stone was used to scrub their skin. Most had never been to school, so they didn't have to be clean for that. As a result of the lack of hygiene, most of them come to us covered in parasites—ringworm and sores—and they don't know anything about washing. Many are actually terrified of getting wet, especially washing their face or head. First, we shave their hair so we can see if there are worms or fungus on their head. Then we teach them how to wash.

It is African tradition to use a basin of water for washing. That way, you don't waste water, since water is an expensive commodity in terms of the strength, time, and the energy it takes to get it from its source, which may be a nearby stream or river, to a home or hut. First, the child sanitizes the basin using a cleaning agent to kill germs, etc. from the child who used it before. We have to teach them how to use soap and a face cloth. We teach them to start at the top of their head and face, and to soap up, covering all areas. Of course, the young ones don't like bathing, and so take many short cuts. They may wash the top of the arm, but not under their arms. There are many challenges, tears, and laughs that go along with learning how to bathe.

When they get used to having water on their skin and being soaped from head to toe, they graduate to using a shower. That's another challenge, because according to African tradition, if you have rain dropping on your head, it exposes you to demons invading your brain. So, many times, you will see people in town walking with plastic shopping bags on their heads. That is not to keep their hair dry, it is to prevent the penetration of demons. So when it comes to showers, that's not just a few raindrops on your head, it is a major downpour of water. Before the children have their first shower, we have a serious talk about these legends and fables about misfortunes and demonic spirits. Those lies have to be removed before the children can shower.

That's the first challenge. The second is to make sure soap is used from head to foot and everywhere between. We also have to make sure the soap is thoroughly rinsed off. Part of a caregiver's responsibility is to make sure each child is soaped and rinsed before they get out of the shower. After they are dry, they rub Vaseline all over their skin to make sure it's moisturized and healthy. Then they get dressed.

This is the routine every morning and evening. The youngest ones go first so they get the hot water. Before long, they get used to showering, and realize they look and smell better when they've had a shower. Taking a shower is just one of many new steps in their new life.

We also have great fun with tooth-brushing. This is a new experience for all of them when they arrive. The younger ones think tooth-brushing is the greatest thrill of the day. They eat the toothpaste instead of using it to clean their teeth. When we have put toothpaste the size of a pea on their brush, we do the whole drill with them. They finally brush their teeth. Then they are so delighted and vigorous with their newly acquired skill, it's a wonder there are any teeth left when they are done.

Cooking

The children learn to do their own cooking, and they are delighted to do that. Mixing and cooking porridge gives them the confidence that they will never again be in a helpless position when it comes to food preparation. They will always know how to prepare food for themselves and others, no matter what circumstance they find themselves in. Even those who cook for a family of five have quite a challenge cooking for a family of forty. They are learning skills with which they can bless others.

Mealtime

One of the favorite routines is eating. We have a ritual about who gets to eat first. In Swazi culture, the enemy of these children has been cruel. Children have little significance—orphaned or not. In most homes, children get the dregs of the meal. Dad gets the choicest piece of meat, followed by the uncles, then the women, and lastly, the children. You can imagine how the bottom of a cooking pot looks and tastes after it has been over a fire for several hours.

We intentionally reverse the order, and start with the youngest first and the eldest last. Just as Jesus said, *"The last shall be first and the first shall be last."* So every day for each meal, we line up in the order of age and sing a prayer together. Actually, we sing a song written by Tracie:

> *Thank you Jesus for this food. Thank you God it tastes so good, please take sickness far away and strengthen me to stand today. Thank you Jesus for this food, thank you God it tastes so good, please take sickness far away and sanctify it in Jesus' name. Amen! Amen!*

The prayer affirms the strength and healing in their bodies, because when they come to us, they all need major healing from malnutrition. Then they receive their food, youngest to oldest. As Director, I am usually the last one to get food. Our meals are composed of the main food groups, but we want to add more vegetables and fruits as time goes on. In God's good time, we will have an abundance of these. Right now, we concentrate on the staples.

After dinner, each child is responsible for washing his or her dish, rinsing it in bleach water to disinfect it. They wipe it dry and stack it on the table before they leave the dining room. Of course, someone has to do the rest of the cleaning of the dining room and the kitchen. It's all good training for life.

Washing Clothes

A skill every African needs to have is the ability to wash clothes clean by hand, so all of the children, including four-year-old Jedidah, wash clothing by hand. The children get outside in the afternoon with their basins of water, and soap and scrub away at their clothing. It's a community time, as, culturally, clothes-washing is done in rivers where everyone gets together and shares news and stories. There have been several studies done where Africans have been put in homes with running water so they didn't have to go to the river to wash clothes. The studies show that the social fabric of the community broke down because there was no community time. So our children have fun with lots of chatting, laughing, telling stories, and sharing their dreams while they get their clothes clean.

Make (mother) Leah makes sure the clothes are clean before they are put on the clothesline to dry. The children try short-cuts, and sometimes young James's clothes actually smell worse after washing them, because he forgets to rinse them out. All of the children are still learning.

Ironing

Ironing is also a part of our culture. When clothing is dried in the sun, there is a certain fly that lays eggs in the clothes. When you wear the clothes that the flies have laid eggs in, the eggs, feeling nice and warm from your body heat, hatch and crawl into the skin. The result is painful infected sores. So it's crucial that every item of clothing, including underwear, be ironed before being worn or being put away in the wardrobe.

Ironing presents a challenge. A little girl like Esther isn't even as tall as the ironing board she needs to use to iron her clothes. A caregiver needs to iron with each little one, keeping their bigger hand over the smaller one. Most of the children can handle ironing safely by the time they are five or six. If they take shortcuts with their ironing task, they quickly experience the consequences of not doing it properly when there is a worm itching beneath their skin. One child, a little older than the others, came to New Hope Centre accustomed to using the traditional wrought iron from the cooking fires. These irons are placed on the fire to heat up, and are cooled off by putting them in a bucket of water. Needless to say, in his first week at New Hope Centre, he put the electric iron and cord into a bucket of water to cool it down. That was the end of that iron, and the beginning of one new item of training on teaching them how to use an iron.

Vegetable Gardening

Africans live close to the soil. Ninety percent of the population of Swaziland is agrarian, living in rural areas. So part of each day is given to the task of maintaining our gardens. We are looking forward to the time when we won't need to buy food. We want to be self-sufficient, but to do so, our children must be able to tend the gardens. A short time ago, a volunteer team came to visit, and planted a huge garden for us. Soon we hope to have funding to build a greenhouse and introduce modern gardening techniques to produce a high yield of vegetables. We would love to use the "tunnels" and drip irrigation.

Each child has his or her own plot to water and care for every day. They have to weed it, put pesticides on it, and when it is harvested, most of what they get will be given to our kitchen so that our family can eat. If we have surplus, we give it away or sell it to the community.

Having something to sell that they have grown themselves encourages and equips the children to become young entrepreneurs. If a child raises tomatoes and we've used all we can, he will sell the surplus at half the market price. That way, we help the impoverished community around us with quality food at reasonable prices. The child is responsible to keep track of his own business, and then we sit down after everything is sold and count the money that has come in.

The young entrepreneur will take ten percent right off the top. This is the tithe. Each child will then make a decision about how the tithe should be used following God's guidelines: *And all the tithe of the land whether seed of the land or fruit of the tree is the Lords. It is holy* (Lev. 27:30). *Bring out the tithe of your produce to the Levite, the stranger (or refugee) the fatherless (orphan) and the widow that God may bless you in all the work of your hand which you do* (Deut. 14.28–29). He can give it as a tithe to the church, or to a widow or fatherless children. He can choose to give it to the poor or to a stranger. Next, he must look at what it cost to raise the crop. After deducting the cost for seedlings, pesticides, and fertilizers, there will be a small profit. We don't charge the child for the salary of the uncle who oversees the gardening project.

It works like this. Suppose Asher was the gardener and he has paid the tithe (ten percent). He then puts aside fifty percent of his earnings for seedlings, fertilizer, etc. to ensure a future harvest. What remains is his. We talk about what he wants. Sometimes, if the gardener is James, he wants five loaves of bread and a big jar of peanut butter. He'll eat peanut butter and bread for the next five days. If it's Joel, he'll save his money for a Discman or an MP3 player so he can listen to his own praise music. We advise them to save some, but they will often want to buy a teddy bear or small car. Little Jesse used his to buy a pair of trainers for another child, who had no shoes. They are still children, after all, and have never been in a position of having their own money to spend. Each child over ten years of age has opened an account at Swazi Bank with ten emalangeni (US$1.50) earning 3 percent interest.

Recreation

Our children have lots of energy. Every school day between 2 p.m. and 2.30 p.m., you will find them doing land exercises to enhance their fitness for swimming. The preschoolers go twice a week to the Cuddle Puddle 12 kilometer away—a sulphur spring of warm water where they learn to swim. The older children are at different levels in swimming training, participating in national and international swim competitions. Caleb, our eldest, has represented Swaziland in Cape Town and Potchefstroom in South Africa and Birmingham in England, and is presently in Niagara in Canada, training for the 2012 Olympics in London with a coach at Brocke University. Noah represented Swaziland in Johannesburg, Durban, and Cape Town in South Africa and Birmingham in England. He is closely followed by Joanna, John, James, Asher, and Elijah, all of whom are in the national swim team for Swaziland. The children learn basketball, netball, volleyball, pool, and soccer, with endless hours of bike riding, jump rope skipping, and cross country jogging. It's important that their daily routine includes a lot of play. They have pets—five dogs, three cats, four chickens, and six cows—that they care for, love, and play with, as well.

Dance and Music

God has ordained praise out of the mouths of babes and infants to silence the angels.

—Psalm 8:12

It gives our Father in heaven great joy to receive praise, honor, and rejoicing from His creation. The password of praise opens the doors to the throne room of God. On Tuesday afternoons, you will find all the children with Miss Tracie, learning joyful music and dance, Israeli-style. On Monday and Wednesday afternoons you will find the various age groups doing classical ballet, hip hop or jazz dance with Miss Steph, a gifted dance teacher from Swaziland, while on Monday and Thursday mornings you will hear the music from the Tabernacle as the ABC's learn the recorder, progress to the keyboards, and then to the instruments they love with Mr. Steven, the music teacher from Uganda. Dr. Paul Opsahl and his wife, Yvonne, visited us in the early days when we had only three children. We shared with them God's desire that we make a joyful noise unto the Lord with drums, tambourines, timbrels, etc.—all that makes for a full orchestra. In the course of months and years, Dr. Opsahl sent us our first container of gifts—an assortment of music instruments, including guitars, violins, flutes, trumpets, French horns, and a small piano. We have yet to have a complete orchestra, but God will move others to collect the instruments that remain silent in attics, basements, and closets as many of life's demands push our talents out of the way.

Jesse is a praiser, and for three years, this little boy prayed for a set of drums. He practiced on everything else in the meantime—the lead in pencils was forever in fragments as pencils or fingers beat out praise on tables, desks, staircases, or tree trunks. Colin, a high school student from Canada, raised the funds and sent them over to Swaziland so Jesse could go shopping and choose his drums. Then Colin came out for the summer to teach him to play.

Gumboot dancing, a specialty developed in the mines of Johannesburg, beats out a rhythm of its own on Fridays and Saturdays. Saturday afternoons, you will hear songs of praise, the Hallelujah Chorus, and other great hymns of praise with the choir master as the Swazi Children's Choir trains. Our aim and delight is to establish a dome of praise as described in Psalm 150.

Praise the Lord!
Praise God in his sanctuary;
Praise Him in his mighty firmament!
Praise Him for his might acts;
Praise Him accordingly to his excellent greatness!
Praise Him with the sound of the trumpet;
Praise Him with the lute and hard!
Praise Him with the timbrel and dance;
Praise Him with string instruments and flutes!
Praise Him with loud cymbals;
Praise Him with clashing cymbals!
Let everything that has breathe praise the Lord.
Praise the Lord.

Holy Ground

When people visit New Hope Centre, they often sense something different about the place. They can see it in our children's faces, but it is not just that. They can feel something different from the ground up. I believe that this is because each day is bookended with praise and worship. When the children come to us, their greatest loss has been the neglect of their spiritual needs. These rescued children's physical and educational needs are so evident that in some children's homes around the country, these are the only needs that are addressed. The spiritual side is not emphasized. However, unless the children's spiritual needs are nurtured, they cannot reach their full potential. We've encouraged the children to learn many songs and many styles of praise and worship—from rousing anthems in SiSwati to contemporary praise in English that has been imported through our volunteers and visitors. We even encourage the children to write their own songs, which Debrah and Ruth do. Miss Tracie and others are continually flowing in a new song (Ps. 149:1–4).

> *Sing to the Lord a new song,*
> *And His praise in the assembly of saints.*
> *Let Israel rejoice in their Maker;*
> *Let the children of Zion be joyful in their King.*
> *Let them praise His name with the dance;*
> *Let them sing praises to Him with the timbrel and harp.*
> *For the Lord takes pleasure in His people;*
> *He will beautify the humble with salvation.*

In salvation is healing, life, satisfaction, contentment, strength, and prosperity. God showed us that a time will come when the sick and lame will come up to our mountain in wheelbarrows and on crutches, but will come down dancing, leaping, and praising God.

Chapter 12

LEADERS TOMORROW OR TODAY?

Amazing grace, how sweet the sound that saved a wretch like me.
I once was lost, but now I'm found, was blind, but now I see.

The number five is the number of grace. As we approached our fifth anniversary on March 24, 2009, we launched the Hope Camps program in a game park called Mlilwane, about seven kilometer from New Hope Centre. We loaded twenty-four children, twelve team members, and twelve South African youth leaders into our purple and yellow buses loaded with tents, clothes, sports equipment, handicraft kits, pots, pans, and food. This was a training camp for all of us as we launched a nationwide psychosocial program for orphans from the north, east, central, and south of Swaziland.

In November 2008, by faith we invited twenty-four head teachers from primary schools in the areas identified with the highest rate of HIV/AIDS incidence. Twenty head teachers came for three days' orientation to the vision God had given for reaching out to the 200,000 orphans in the country. There are organizations, both NGO and Government, that provide soup kitchens, and OVC (Orphans and Vulnerable Children) care points. These mostly focus on helping children with food, clothing, and a place to hang out during the day. Our focus is to address the psychosocial needs of these children; to provide a means for them to deal with the process of grief and loss recovery, and the process of developing life skills and resilience.

The problems we have seen and experienced throughout Swaziland largely pertain to children losing hope, becoming trapped in the resentment or anger of being orphaned or abandoned by adults, relatives, and caregivers, or the depression and despair of losing everyone or everything they have known.

Our children know very well the feelings, terrors, and struggles these children face. Our children are committed and determined to intervene and make a difference in the lives of others. From the very first year we started the home, our children prepared skits, dramas, dances, and songs to share in churches or schools around Swaziland. Our objective was:

1. To make known God's will and purpose for each and every child who is part of a nation that is the "apple of God's eye" in Africa.
2. To establish with God's Word the truth that will bring a lively hope into the lives of children who have every reason to give up in life.
3. To share and encourage other children in basic life skills, nutrition, hygiene, and the maintenance of a healthy positive attitude to life.
4. To educate children in sexuality, appropriate and inappropriate touch and behavior, educating them towards premarital sexual abstinence and faithfulness in marriage by learning skills of respect, intimacy, and integrity in relationships.

We seek God for what is on His heart to meet the need of the hour in each school, church, or community, then we script and choreograph a twenty- to thirty-minute presentation. To reach some schools in time for assembly, we would have to leave home at 4 A.M. and return around 4 P.M., having ministered in six to eight schools in one day. Now, we are able to work in four teams of six children each, and we have targeted twenty-four primary schools around Swaziland each year, beginning in 2009. Miss Rachael from Australia is our coordinator, and we are praying for funding for another three vehicles and another three coordinators to be able to grow in the next five years to one hundred twenty schools.

There are generally between 350 to 1,350 students in each school. This means that as we go to each school three times per year, we cover thousands of miles (or kilometer) each year and reach tens of thousands of primary and elementary children between the ages of five and twenty-five.

The second phase of intervention in each school is the training of a team of six adults to work with the OVC's throughout the year. Two teachers, two youth leaders, and two caregivers selected by the head teachers or school staff are being trained at New Hope Centre to make the school environment a resource for caring for the whole person, to enable the children to grow up to be overcomers and contribute responsibly to the future of our nation. The focus in preparing teachers has been to equip them to identify children struggling with their circumstances, to give rudimentary counseling to their students, and to support them in the event that a child's challenge needs to be referred to more skilled counseling intervention. The youth leaders are trained and supported to convene weekly Hope Clubs for discussions, help with homework and life skills, make home visits, and be a friend and mentor to the OVC's. The caregivers (Hope Helpers) are trained to be aware of the assistance that children can obtain through NGO's and government agencies, and to serve as advocates, helping them with their legal rights to their homes, their inheritance, and the like. This, then, serves as a safety net to ensure that our nation will never face a scenario where children "home alone" are vulnerable to the depravity of mankind, being mindful that "what we do to children today is what they will do to society tomorrow."

The third intervention is a one-week psychosocial camp. Our children were trained in April 2009 to direct, manage, and head a seven-day psychosocial camp. Miss Rachael, our Children's Ministry Coordinator, together with Miss Tracie, our Education Manager, and Miss Zanele, our Education Administrator, with a team of twelve youth leaders from South Africa and twelve team members from New Hope Centre, formed the support system for our children. Once our children went through their own training in April, they led a camp in July 2009, training youth leaders from the twenty targeted schools followed by a camp with one hundred thirty-five participants, including sixty orphaned children (three from each of the twenty schools).

These camps have been developed over the past five years by Auntie Heather and myself together with many others. Our purpose is to make a difference in the life of an orphaned child identified by each school as "most-in-need-of-help" because they are becoming overwhelmed by their circumstances. We prepare plenty of good wholesome food and lots of fun and games, as well as serious "Dream Team" work, where the children work through *My Hero Book*. This facilitates discussions about their life stories, their challenges, fears, monsters, hopes, and expectations in life. They play sports and overcome fears by doing things they have never done before, like riding a horse, swimming in a swimming pool, or climbing a sheer rock face mountain. We were able to use the *25-Item Resilience Scale* test as a pre- and post-test to measure to some degree the success of the camp. Sixty percent of the campers' resilience score improved and in thirty percent, the level of resilience improved. The test will be repeated after three months to ascertain the sustainability of their newly-acquired attitudes and emotional strengths.

In the years to come, we shall run a camp inviting three children from each school in the spring vacation around April and the fall vacation around September, and in July, at the time of the National Somhlolo Festival of Praise, we will have one week training new youth leaders and a second week bringing three children from twenty new schools into our program. Our commitment to each school will be for five years. Thereafter, we hope each school will have a Hope Centre, providing psychosocial support and maintaining the seven dimensions of Hope Clubs and Hope Camps. As I write this very afternoon, Tirzah and Noah are launching the first Hope Club for orphan children on the backside of our Bethany Mountain.

There is a chart included in this book, titled "Hope Camp Leaders 2009" that shows our six main leaders and their responsibilities and also shows the venue where each of our children worked for the camp. Take a moment to meet the Abraham children in their roles as leaders enabling other children to overcome these challenges in life with a lively hope and trust in our loving and competent heavenly Father.

The inauguration teams of youth leaders were courageous and enthusiastic. International volunteers were from South Africa and Canada this first year. May God continue to inspire and recruit His beloved young people from the nations of the world. Look into your own heart as you read this, and see if you sense a desire or quickening to be a part of saving a nation that, without your help, could be in danger of extinction from the family of nations on the planet earth. We are deeply committed to Jehovah Yahweh, the giver and sustainer of all that has life and breath, and we believe passionately in God's destiny for this tiny nation to become renowned in the earth due to the divine intervention of His almighty love through those who allow Him to stir and motivate them to make a difference in ending a nation's death sentence and igniting a testimony of glorious abundant life.

CONCLUSION

After reading this book, can you see why we believe God's Word that *a little child will lead them*? Can you see why we believe that for Swaziland, these little ones are the hope for the future? Can you feel the hope that it will be these children who grow up to ensure that their nation reaches its destiny—which we believe is to become the pulpit of Africa?

But there is an even greater significance to the "little ones." Why did Jesus put such importance on childlike faith? I believe it is because of what is in a child. Children have a deeper consciousness of who God is and what heaven is all about. Little children easily trust our Heavenly Father. They understand His love. The traditions and expectations of man have not yet taken root in them. The truth that is Jesus is close to them. The Bible says they are so important that their angels have perpetual access to Almighty God as they do this assignment of ministry to these children.

One More Story of God's Care

Let me tell you one more amazing story that shows how God cares for these children, and how He intervenes on a daily basis to help these children become leaders of their nation.

When we opened our home in 2004, June McKinney prophesied that someone in this home would bring back gold medals in swimming from the Olympics. Well, that didn't seem like anything that was remotely possible. But it was on God's heart, and He is never limited by our thinking. Here's what happened.

Shortly after the centre opened, a mud-covered Land Rover drove up, and a young man jumped out. He said he had come from Swaziland's Olympic Swimming Committee. He wanted to create a swimming program to include orphans. He offered to train four staff members to be coaches, and he arranged for us to have free swimming time at the local pool—a hot-springs-fed pool at the Royal Swazi Convention Centre.

So twice a week, we packed up our brood (eight children at the time) and made the twelve-kilometer trek to the pool. It was a clean pool, not a muddy pond behind a mud dam somewhere in the bush. God catapulted us into our first sports activity. We chose our teachers and caregivers, who then passed beginner and intermediate coaching courses. They had never been in a pool before this time. Some had never been in more water than you can put in a tub. It was quite an adventure for us all.

In the second year of swim training, the children began to compete in Swazi competitions. One by one, they walked off with gold, silver, and bronze medals and qualified for the next level.

One of our children, Noah, is particularly gifted as a swimmer, and qualified all the way through to the national team to represent Swaziland in a regional swim gala in Johannesburg.

So this child, who had never been in a pool before we began his training, represented our country among eight others and came back with a silver medal. We know that one day we will see an Olympic gold medal in our home.

A year later, a visitor from the UK spent an afternoon with us and heard about the swimming. He returned home and arranged for Noah and Caleb to spend the month of February in Birmingham, England, training with the youngsters for the 2012 Olympics. Their coach, however, was concerned about Caleb's eyes. He had a condition that complicated his depth and distance perception. So he compensated by slowing down just before he touched the wall. Chris, the coach, talked with his friend, an optician, who tested Caleb's eyes. Surgery was needed, but in Swaziland no one had the skills or equipment, and in South Africa we would have to raise the funds for private health care. But God was preparing the provision. John, the optician, had a colleague who is an eye surgeon and was his friend in University. So he offered his professional skills as a gift. The surgeon then negotiated with the anesthesiologist and medical centre to do the operation. Ralph Bromley and Janine Maxwell helped raise the funds to cover the transport, accommodation, and hospital bills. Caleb healed well, and was able to go with Noah to Birmingham, England, for training.

They came back from England, and, in March, flew with Miss Tracie to represent Swaziland in Cape Town. Later, Caleb went with the Swaziland Sports Association to the Southern African Region 6 Games and represented Swaziland. He came back sharing that they were treated like kings. Each had a BMW car and two security police assigned to transport and escort them everywhere. This former orphan and street child now stood on a podium receiving medals while the national anthem played.

SWAZILAND'S NATIONAL ANTHEM

SiSwati

Nkulunkulu Mnikati
wetibusiso temaSwati;
Siyatibonga tonkhe
tinhlanhla,
Sibonga iNgwenyama yetfu,
Live netintsaba nemifula.

Busisa tiphatsimandla
takaNgwane
Nguwe wedvwa Somandla
wetfu;
Sinike kuhlakanipha
lokungenabucili
Simise usicinise, Simakadze.

English

O Lord our God, bestower of the
blessings of the Swazi;
We give Thee thanks for all our good
fortune;
We offer thanks and praise for our King
And for our fair land, its hills and rivers.

Thy blessings be on all rulers of our
country;
Might and power are Thine alone;
We pray Thee to grant us wisdom
without deceit or malice.
Establish and fortify us, Lord
Eternal.

So we've begun, and there is so much more to be done. It is our dream to have the first orchestra in Swaziland—one that can make a joyful noise to the Lord. We started with recorders, a piano, a guitar, and African drums. Once the children mastered these instruments, they moved on to flutes and violins. We prayed that more instruments would come and more teachers who can teach those instruments to our children. We received a small container load of our first used orchestral instruments, collected by Dr. Paul Opsahl in Ohio. We are trusting God for more.

Along with musical instruments, several of the children are already accomplished dancers. A Canadian volunteer, Miss Lindsay, established the Hosanna School of Dance, and Miss Shannon from the USA came for a few months and taught

Celtic dancing. We train the older children or more skilled dancers, and they teach others in the home and community who want to give honor to God in praise and worship. Whether through ballet or hip-hop, we believe that our children will bring the power and presence of God to us as they dance.

Dancers, doctors, missionaries, or teachers; we don't know what our children will become. We just know that they each have a destiny that will help save their nation. Their destinies are not up to us. They rest in God's hands. So far, God is helping us give them what they will need to become tomorrow's leaders. Our job is to build skills, character, confidence, and spiritual strength, and also to give them the knowledge that they are chosen, loved, and highly valuable in God's eyes and ours. As they walk in the will of God and His manifold wisdom, they have full confidence and boldness. Others will trust them, and they will become the leaders this nation so desperately needs.

Shalom

Hope Camp

Caleb Abraham
Camp Director

Noah Abraham
Camp Manager

Tirzah Abraham
Camp Manager

Caleb Abraham *Pastor Mentor*	**Debrah Abraham** *Pastor Mentor*	**Phoebe Abraham** *Pastor Mentor*
Zadok Abraham *Dance/Drama* *Team Leader*	**Zodwa Dlamini** *Dance/Drama* *Team Leader*	**Philippa Abraham** *Dance/Drama* *Team Leader*
Debrah Abraham *Sports / Dream* *Team Leaders*	**Samuel Abraham** *Sports / Dream* *Team Leaders*	**James Abraham** *Sports / Dream* *Team Leaders*
Lydia Abraham *Bead Work*	**Asher Abraham** *Bead Work*	**Ruth Abraham** *Bead Work*
Caleb Abraham *Worship Team*	**Anastasia Abraham** *Worship Team*	**Phoebe Abraham** *Worship Team*
Tirzah Abraham *Hairdressing* *Team Leader*	**James Abraham** *Hairdressing* *Team Leader*	**Samuel Abraham** *Horse Riding* *Supervisor*

eaders 2009

Suzzanna Abraham
Camp Director

Anastasia Abraham
Camp Administrator

Zipporah Abraham
Camp Administrator

Suzzanna Abraham *Pastor Mentor*	**Noah Abraham** *Counsellor*	**Anastasia Abraham** *Counsellor*
Esther Abraham *Dance/Drama Team Leader*	**Joel Abraham** *Sound Engineer*	**Elijah Abraham** *Sound Engineer*
John Abraham *Sports / Dream Team Leaders*	**Joel Abraham** *Wire Work Team Leader*	**Elijah Abraham** *Wire Work Team Leader*
Jesse Abraham *Body Movement*	**Phoebe Abraham** *Body Movement*	**Tabitha Abraham** *Pom Pom + Cards*
Jesse Abraham *Worship Team*	**Phoebe Abraham** *Puppeteer*	**Joanna Abraham** *Puppeteer*
Debrah Abraham *Horse Riding Supervisor*	**John Abraham** *Horse Riding Supervisor*	**Joanna Abraham** *Music*

SPONSORING A CHILD AT NEW HOPE CENTRE

Sponsoring a child for $/£30, 50, 100 or 120 will provide some of their following needs:

- Nutritious food
- Medical health care
- Clothing
- Running of the home - water, caregivers, electricity, gas for cooking, security etc.
- Education - school fees, uniform, books, tuition fees, sports activities.

A gift of $/£150 for a starter pack will provide a new child at New Hope Centre a mattress, set of toiletries, bedding set, towel set, underwear, blanket, duvet, pillow, school kit, clothes etc.

How can I communicate with the child I sponsor?

You are encouraged to pray for the child and to develop a relationship through correspondence. You may write to the child you are sponsoring as often as you like. When you write, the child will benefit from knowing that someone in addition to their New Hope Centre family really cares for them. Your words of encouragement will make a difference to the child in many ways, and the more you write, the more they will reap the benefits of your relationship. As you write and share your joys, overcomings, loves, and all your life's experiences, this will build joy, hope, and love in the child's life. We also encourage you to send the child photos of yourself or your family, which they will treasure and keep in their "memory boxes."

[Please note that all correspondence is first read by a team member. We ask that you do not make any mention of being orphaned in your correspondence, as this triggers loss once again.]

Will the child write to me?

Every year you will receive from the sponsored child:

- Thank-you card
- Christmas card
- Updated photo of the child on a bookmark calendar
- Annual newsletter from New Hope Centre.

The child will write to you twice a year with the help of their teachers. Letter-writing is developmental for the child, as it improves their basic literacy, self-awareness, and ability to put thoughts and feelings into words. As you exchange correspondence with the child, your relationship will grow and develop. The child will also develop a sense of confidence and self-worth with the love you express through letters and prayers.

Can I send gifts to the sponsored child?

We encourage you to give additional monetary gifts to the child for special occasions, to address specific needs, or simply as an act of love. These gifts are another effective way for you to reinforce your care, commitment, and support to the child.

One hundred percent of the gift amounts go to your sponsored child. To make certain that these funds are used appropriately, team members will accompany the child shopping so that they learn about budgeting, making wise choices, and preparing a shopping list of needs and wants.

You may also send a gift to your sponsored child's community ministry. With your monetary gift of $/£20 to $/£300, the child and the team from New Hope Centre will buy items for orphan-headed families or widows in our community, such as blankets, livestock, and food supplies. We will work closely with the family to determine the greatest need, and then purchase items accordingly. All family gift amounts go to the needy family, and your gifts empower your sponsored child to learn compassionate giving.

You may choose to send a gift to your sponsored child by mail. Please mark on the item "GIFT AID FOR ORPHANS," and on the custom form please mark "NO RESALE VALUE." Also, please do not put any value on the package, as it is a gift. If you use courier, please include 14% of the value as cash inside the package for us to pay for customs; otherwise we will be charged.

Is there anything I cannot send to the child I sponsor?

As a sponsor, you have many opportunities to correspond with the child, and we encourage you to do so. We ask that when you communicate with the sponsored child that you will provide comments and materials consistent with Christian values and philosophies. Please do not send comments or materials that:

- Have symbols of ghosts, Spiderman, snakes, witches, five-pointed stars, etc.;
- No candy or sweets (for dental reasons!);
- Anything that might be considered inappropriate in our culture;
- Anything that might promote lifestyle choices that we view as unhealthy and inconsistent with biblically-based lifestyles or otherwise inappropriate for the child.

What happens if I discontinue my sponsorship?

You may choose to discontinue your sponsorship at any time. We ask that you notify us by e-mailing us at newhope@ africanonline.co.sz. We understand that circumstances can sometimes change. However, we need to let the child know, so that they are not longing and hoping for something that is no more, and so that another sponsor can be found for your sponsored child.

Your relationship with your sponsored child makes you a very important person who has a significant role in their life, particularly as it gives the child value as a person knowing that there is someone who believes in them enough to support them. You stand alongside pastors, teachers, family, and friends who are taking an active role in encouraging and developing the child to become a confident, biblically-sound leader of tomorrow.

Thank you for wishing to sponsor a precious child of God at New Hope Centre. Please complete the Child Sponsor Form and e-mail/send it to us. If you have any further questions, please contact us at:

Postal Address:
New Hope Centre, PO Box 384,
Manzini M200, Swaziland
Tel No: +268 5185304
E-mail: newhope@africaonline.co.sz

New Hope Centre

P O Box 384, Manzini M200, Swaziland
Phone: (+268) 518 5304   Fax: (+268) 505 3338
Email: newhope@africaonline.co.sz.

Child Sponsor Form

You have an opportunity to give a child at New Hope Centre hope, and to become a very important

person who has a significant role in their life. You can support the child by giving a regular amount

each month, making a one-off contribution or providing some other resource that may be needed,

such as supplies, equipment or practical skills.

I would like to sponsor [*child's name*]..

☐ Child Sponsorship	$/£30 pm	☐ Child Sponsorship	$/£50 pm
☐ Child Sponsorship	$/£100 pm	☐ Child Sponsorship	$/£120 pm
☐ Educate a Child	$/£30pm	☐ Starter Pack	$/£150pm
☐ Child Sponsorship (other)	$/£.......pm	☐ Single Donation	$/£.......pm

(Please complete where blank if you are giving an amount that is other than stated).

PLEASE COMPLETE IN CAPTIAL LETTERS

Title (Mr/Mrs/Ms etc) .... First Name... Surname...............................

Address: ....

.... Post Code.................................

Tel Home........................... Cell..................................... Email...

Signature..   Date........../............./...........

Please see overleaf for methods of payment if you wish to sponsor a child.

PTO

" Out of the mouths of babes and infants you have perfected praise." Psalms 8:2
"Indvumiso yemandla akho, uyibeke emilonyeni yebanfwana." Tihlabelelo 8:2

METHOD OF PAYMENT

- **Tax Deductible** – Please contact respective Hope For The Nations office, explaining your wish to sponsor a child at New Hope Centre and giving name of sponsored child as a reference:

Canada Office

Hope For The Nations
2041 Harvey Avenue
Kelowna BC
V1Y 6G7, CANADA.
Tel No: +1 250 712 2007
Email: support@hopeforthenations.com
Website: www.hopeforthenations.com

USA Office

Hope for the Nations USA
Suite #500-7729
East Greenway Road, Scottsdale
AZ 85260, USA
Tel No: +1 480 882 0800
Email: admin@hopeforthenations.com
Website: www.hopeforthenations.com

UK Office

Hope For The Nations Childrens Charity
23 Caldervale
Orton Longueville
Peterborough, PE2 7HX
UNITED KINGDOM
Tel No: +44 (0) 01733 237377
Email: info@hftn.co.uk
Website: www.hftn.co.uk

- **Cheque** payable to "New Hope Centre" by mail. Please mark clearly on back of cheque 'Name of Child' you wish to sponsor.

New Hope Centre
PO Box 384
Manzini M200
SWAZILAND

- **Electronic Transfer.** Please mark as a reference 'Name of Child' you wish to sponsor and email to confirm when transaction completed at newhope@africaonline.co.sz so we can look out for it.

Account Name:	New Hope Centre
Branch Name:	Nedbank Manzini
Brach Number:	36 02 64
Account Number:	040000161219
SWIFT Code:	NESWSZMX

" Out of the mouths of babes and infants you have perfected praise." Psalms 8:2
"Indvumiso yemandla akho, uyibeke emilonyeni yebanfwana." Tihlabelelo 8:2

How to Volunteer

If you would like to volunteer at New Hope Centre, please contact us at:

New Hope Center
PO Box 384
Manzini M200
Swaziland

Or e-mail us at New Hope Centre
newhope@africaonline.co.sz

We need: registered nurses, music teachers, children's pastors, primary school teachers with ACE (Accelerated Christian Education) experience, sports teachers, dance teachers, psychotherapists or counsellors, maintenance and site managers, car and vehicle maintenance specialists, and heavy duty drivers for transporting kids in buses.

If you have any of these skills and would like to volunteer from two weeks to six months, we would like to hear from you.

For more information on New Hope Centre, go to **www.newhopeswaziland.com**

New Hope Centre
PO Box 384, Manzini M200, Swaziland
Phone: (+268) 518 5304
Fax: (+268) 505 3338
E-mail: newhope@africaonline.co.sz.

Book Order Form

If you would like to order more copies of
A Little Child Shall Lead Them, please contact us at:

NHCWise@gmail.com

You can also purchase books online at:
http://www.newhopeswaziland.com/resources.asp

Forms of payment:
Paypal, all major credit cards, checks, and money orders.

WinePressPublishing
Your Book, Defined.

To order additional copies of this book call:
1-877-421-READ (7323)
or please visit our website at
www.WinePressbooks.com

If you enjoyed this quality custom-published book,
drop by our website for more books and information.

www.winepresspublishing.com
"Your partner in custom publishing."